THE KASHMIR NARRATIVE

Time For Vigorous Adaptations

THE KASHMIR NARRATIVE

Time For Vigorous Adaptations

Lt Gen Gautam Banerjee, PVSM, AVSM, YSM (Retd)

Foreword by

Gen N C Vij, PVSM, UYSM, AVSM (Retd)
Director, Vivekananda International Foundation

Vivekananda International Foundation
New Delhi

PENTAGON PRESS

The Kashmir Narrative: Time For Vigorous Adaptations
Lt Gen Gautam Banerjee
Vivekananda International Foundation, New Delhi

ISBN 978-81-8274-899-6

First Published in 2017

Published by
PENTAGON PRESS
206, Peacock Lane, Shahpur Jat,
New Delhi-110049
Phones: 011-64706243, 26491568
Telefax: 011-26490600
email: rajan@pentagonpress.in
website: www.pentagonpress.in

Printed at Avantika Printers Private Limited.

CONTENTS

FOREWORD

The Vale of Kashmir is in broil once again, just when the normalcy appeared to be returning. The Pakistani establishment has heavily interfered in the affairs of Kashmir and has been pursuing the course of proxy war to keep Kashmir disturbed. As a matter of fact, the area which is affected is only the Valley. The rest of the areas have more or less returned to normal lives. However, this time, there also appears to be alienation in the minds of the people, especially in the youth. The Government of India should be fully aware of this and must evolve a strategy to meet the aspirations of the Kashmiris.

Taking cognisance of the ground realities, policy measures and implementation mechanisms that prevail, we in the Vivekananda International Foundation (VIF) have been continuously analysing the situation in the Kashmir Valley. This publication, *The Kashmir Narrative: Time For Vigorous Adaptations* is one such effort. It is not necessarily the VIF's fixed view, nor does it claim to be the final word.

It is argued here that the Indian Union's policy of exclusivity of the Kashmir Valley combined with its favour of local perfidy has allowed the Kashmir problem to fester for far too long. It is therefore very essential that the Government adopts all measures at its command and apply a well rounded policy to tackle the problem in the Valley.

I hope the descriptions and discussions contained in the following pages would find salience in dealing with this perennial problem that saddles a democratic and peace loving India.

General N C Vij, PVSM, UYSM, AVSM (Retd)
Director, Vivekananda International Foundation
May, 2017, New Delhi

THE KASHMIR NARRATIVE: TIME FOR VIGOROUS ADAPTATIONS

"There comes a time when one must take a position that is neither safe, nor politic, nor popular, but he must take it because conscience tells him it is right."

– Martin Luther King Jr., the great promoter of peace.

THE THEME

It is a sign of decay when the majesty of the State is mocked by brash celebrations of mob disloyalty while a most benevolent constitutional authority, ever ready to nurture the society, stands watching vilified and hapless. That is the warning for the Indian Union to shed pretensions and adapt to new initiatives and fresh strategies to deal with anti-state disorder.

The never-ending cycles of bloody militancy that engulfs the Kashmir Valley is instigated by a habitually irrepressible external enemy. In active collaboration is a class of traitors who have used religious subterfuge to be in position to call the shots in a society which has been left vulnerable by the Union under a lopsided pretext of democratic autonomy and individual liberty. Waning and waxing, that tumult remains unabated for the past seven decades; in fact it has exacerbated, and there is no end in sight. The fact is that the Kashmir Valley is in the grip of secessionist criminals. The issue is, how long would the Indian Union put up with this kind of anti-national affront? Do we expect this seven decade long attempt to disintegrate India to go on endlessly, or do we girdle up to end this evil at some point in time?

The time has come to apply our long administrative experience and proven military acumen to invigorate our strategy of defeating secessionist militancy in the Kashmir Valley. It is time for the Indian Union to elevate its somewhat tentative relationship with the Kashmiri society and establish intimate connection between the State and the Kashmiri citizens. To conclusively end the ever-escalating environment of treason and bloodshed, the Indian State must invigorate its strategy to defeat the secessionist militancy by the adoption of harder and telling administrative, civic and military measures.

This paper contends that the secessionist rhetoric, even if it is hollow and impractical, has found deep roots due to the Indian Union's distancing itself from the people of Kashmir and leaving the management of the State to incompetent politicians, religious fanatics and corrupt tricksters. It examines the tumult in the Kashmir Valley from its origins to propose adoption of extraordinary measures with the purpose of rooting it out rather than just stalling it endlessly. In that context, it proposes immediate extraordinary, albeit temporary, measures like reorganisation of governing establishment, better and effective governance, and more robust police action, while taking the possible negatives in stride. There cannot be full stops in an endeavour to preserve national integrity.

PREAMBLE

Test of Nationhood

The entire State of Jammu and Kashmir (J&K), and Ladakh, as it existed at the time of its accession to Independent India in 1947, is a part of India. In contest are the Pakistanis and Kashmir Valley based bigots who claim that with its majority of 'fellow' Muslims, the State of J&K must be a part of Pakistan. At the time of its accession to India in October 1947, the Kashmiri society suffered no such illusion, particularly after having been subjected to rapine at the hands of Pakistani army-tribal marauders sent in to seize Kashmir by force. Seven decades down the line, as one would think, all Indian citizens would have appreciated the blessings of independence, democracy and national integration – and so do everything to consolidate the Union. In case of the Kashmir Valley, a small but significant part of the State of J&K, the tendency however has been the opposite.

As a result of incessant Pakistani propaganda of falsehood and hate, and the resultant consolidation of religious fundamentalism in the Valley, there are reasons to believe that India's position on the invented 'dispute' over the status of the J&K State stands somewhat marred. At the global level, serious appreciation of India's cause against Pakistan-staged secessionist militancy in the Kashmir Valley appears to be clouded by a weariness wrung by Pakistan's drone-like propaganda of lies and slander, and its propensity to military aggression and nuclear placard waiving.

Recently, anti-national armed uprising in the Vale of Kashmir had escalated to an unprecedented level. It is only a matter of seasons when, bolstered with regular quantum's of poison pumped up from Pakistan and strengthening of local religious and money-making vested interests, the tumult could keep escalating for the world to be further misled and Pakistan to hammer its next blow upon the roots of Indian nationhood. Obviously, our policy in assimilating the people of the Valley has failed to deliver – seven decades is a long time to accept that. Time has therefore come to devise new approaches to prevent the falsehood of 'Muslim' cause for 'liberation from non-Muslim rule' from blowing away our democratic, secular, all-inclusive way of life. And that purpose is better served by revisiting the problem from its roots upwards.

> ... our policy in assimilating the people of the Valley has failed to deliver – seven decades is a long time to accept that ... time to devise new approaches to prevent the falsehood of 'Muslim' cause for 'liberation from non-Muslim rule' from blowing away our democratic, secular, all-inclusive way of life ...

It is therefore time to reiterate, more firmly and demonstratively, to the people of Kashmir Valley, Pakistan and the world, that accession of the entire State of J&K into the Indian Union is, and must, remain a settled issue. The endless, and now escalatory, armed secessionism in the Kashmir Valley makes it imperative to reiterate that stance. Having in our historic past repeatedly suffered the consequences of seeking terms with external aggression and internal subversion, wisdom leaves India with no scope but to repudiate any notions of compromise in this respect.

It is proposed to delve into the matter in three Parts. In Part 1, the situation that gave rise to the secessionist tendency in the Kashmir Valley would be recapitulated from a so far dormant angle. The following part will be a factual description of the current situation to point out the grave danger that secessionism in Kashmir Valley spells against India's national integrity. In Part 3, possible steps, that could be considered to invigorate those which are already in practice, to the conclusive integration of the State of J&K into the Union, would be examined.

PART 1: RISE OF SECESSIONIST TENDENCY IN THE KASHMIR VALLEY

The Partition: Coalescence of Religious Bigotry and Imperialist Frustration

It all began with the vision of a 'Muslim' Pakistan which had to be 'superior' to 'Hindu' India in all respects. According to this vision, Muslims were the rightfully ordained rulers of the Indian sub-continent whereas the Hindus were mere serfs, so to say. So it was unthinkable for Muslim aristocrats who had seized the reigns of Muslim leadership of undivided India, and whom the native Muslims accepted as such on grounds of religious solidarity, to live under Hindu majority rule.[1] At the other end, among the British imperialist ruling class was conjured an intense 'Churchillan' hatred of the Indians who were accused of 'prising out the jewel from the British Crown' and of triggering the destruction of an Empire over which "the Sun never set". Both notions were false of course.[2] But then, notions of grandeur and hegemony are not to be satiated by logical reasoning, just as self-absolving perceptions are liable to prevail over rational introspection.

> ... 'claimed' Kashmir's merger with Pakistan on the premise that this Muslim majority state could not be a part of 'Hindu' India ... that flawed idea – dismissed with due disdain by the majority of Muslims themselves who chose to keep their home in secular India – marked the beginning of that 'problem' and the 'dispute' that goes on ceaselessly, with neither settlement, nor peace in sight ...

That was so when in 1947, the surreptitious, recently revealed, Jinnah-Churchill scheming took shape. Parts of the

Princely State of J&K – Gilgit, Hunza, Skardu etc. where the people had little affiliation to the idea of Pakistan – were handed over to Pakistan. Soon, Kashmir was invaded by British acquiesced and Pakistan Army led tribal hoards, and that triggered the State's accession – for its own safety – to the Indian Union. Next, poised at the point of stalling that invasion, India was nudged to bank its interests to a yet fledging United Nations (UN) which chose to go by British advise on this matter. British endearment of Pakistan continues to date, if in more subtle ways, and it being the predecessor power, British opinion is taken seriously by most of the Western World. Traces of that endearment survive today when in a world dominated by Western Powers, Pakistan's 'underdog' pretensions finds more acceptability; its subterfuge is indulged, its villainy is 'winked at' and its flouting of international norms are let pass. An intransigent state is thus offered finances and arms ostensibly to 'control' its self-nurtured terrorist assets, its nuclear proliferation is tolerated, its genocides are overlooked and its sabotage of neighbours' peace and stability are acquiesced to – a pigmy is even hyphened with India!

The newly carved State of Pakistan, in having to sanctify its 'two-nation theory' that led to the bloody vivisection of a great Indian sub-continent, contrived to adopt two steps to find its legitimacy. One was the institutional vilification of anything Indian -'Hindu' purportedly – in order to ingrain its coming generations with innate dislike, if not hatred, of India. The upper riparian status of Kashmir and Ladakh that could reportedly parch out Pakistan, added to that innate India-animus. The other step was to anoint itself as a patron of global Islamic *Ummah*. On the first count, success remained but stymied by the sublime influence of noble Indian native culture, while on the second count, Pakistan's pretensions amused the entrenched Arab 'custodians' of Islam but did little else. Pakistan was thus left with no option but to build its nascent nationhood on anti-Indian platform.[3]

Post-Partition Paradox

The geo-political status of the Kashmir Valley is stated to be a 'problem'. Right from the time the Islamic State of Pakistan was carved out of India, leaders of Muslim Pakistan have 'claimed' Kashmir's merger with Pakistan on the premise that this Muslim majority state could not be a part of 'Hindu' India when the purpose of partitioning it was to give Indian Muslims their own space to chart their destiny 'free from domination of Hindu majority' (sic). It is that flawed idea – dismissed with due disdain by the majority of Muslims themselves who chose to keep their home in secular India – which marked the beginning of that 'problem' and the 'dispute' that goes on ceaselessly, with neither settlement, nor peace in sight.

At the beginning, India refused to acknowledge Kashmir as a 'disputed territory', sticking to a position that the accession of the Princely State of J&K was legally irrefutable and final. India's stance was built around the fact that the accession drew its sanctity from the same 'Independence of India Act, 1947' which was instrumental in creation of Pakistan. The Act itself was enacted by the British Crown's Parliament which, being vested with British India's sovereignty by international law, had the competence to do so, and that was duly accepted by Congress as well as the Muslim League, the parties representing the two successor States. Questioning the accession was therefore like questioning the partition and creation of Pakistan itself and the various 'awards' that went with it. Besides, India was a secular nation and therefore any further vivisection on religious basis was nothing but an assault upon the foundations of her nationhood.

In 1948, convinced of the legal position and expectation of a fair deal from the newly and hopefully created world body, India was led into seeking the intervention of the UN. Of course, concern of depleting war wherewithal and a novice national leadership's innocent distaste for military action clinched the decision. Furthermore, what remained mostly unstated was that in appreciating the difficulties of assimilating the ethnically and socially disparate population of that part of J&K that was left in Pakistan's occupation, particularly that of the historically uncontrollable tribal regions, the Indian Government found it expedient to stop at what territory had been freed from Pakistan's invasion. It then bet upon the wisdom of world powers to settle the rest of the territory more or less in favour of India – peacefully. In the event, the result was the opposite. Pakistan retains, and gradually gobbles up its already occupied territories while perpetrating bloodshed to wrest the rest of it from India. All this while, the world powers, unable to find a way out, stand watching pacified with a situation of 'no war – no peace' at hand.

The paradox would remain half told unless a demonic understanding that is promoted amongst a large section of Pakistani constituencies is pointed out. Rumbustious conveners of Islamist-Pakistan hot-heads perceive it to be a divine right of the Muslims – Pakistani Muslims, not the Indian ones, of course – to 'rule from Delhi's Red Fort', and are disturbed by Indian Muslims owning up their secular environment. Thus there are the visible symptoms of a dream of seeing to the disintegration of India, to gain parity and then superiority, before the self-certified 'heirs' of Ghori, Ghazni and Babur might banish the Hindu *kafirs* and regain their 'right' to the Indian throne. They are right, of course – secession of Kashmir would be the trigger for another break-up of the 'Indian Empire', so to state.[4]

> ... to retain the Kashmiri people's confidence upon the democratic credibility of the Indian Union, the national level polity at the Centre, and in most instances even at the State levels, abstained from establishing the tradition of intimate politician-constituency relationships with the common man ...

Obviously in the foreseeable future, neither its Government nor the bigot majority in Pakistan are likely to be cured of that cognitively ingrained animosity against India. Three military aggressions, infliction of numerous violent actions in Jammu, Kashmir and Ladakh, sabotage and subversion in the rest of India, diplomatic abuse, trade barriers etc. are the manifestations of that impellence. It is against such a compelling hostility that a secular, democratic and much challenged India must find peace, stability and progress to chart her destiny.

Debase of State Apparatus

Following the accession of the State of J&K, began the Indian Union's democratic assimilation of the people of the Kashmir Valley – the rest of the State – Jammu, South of Pir Panjal Ranges and Ladakh – needed no prompting to do so. First, in expectation of their ownership of the Indian Constitution, the Indian Union acceded to the application of certain 'special provisions' for the State of J&K. Next, allowance of socio-economic and political advantages, purportedly to keep the people from getting estranged from the Indian nationhood, was turned into a branded policy of the Indian State. Thus over the decades following that secular accession – even if that was purely to their self-interests – the Kashmiri polity had been adulated rather well by a gratuitous Indian Union. As a result, the people of J&K, particularly those living in the Kashmir Valley, enjoy economic, medical, educational and infrastructural advantages much in excess of the citizens of many parts of the rest of India.

Further, succumbing to a combination of emotional and partisan predilections, that was cleverly motivated by local people's spokespersons, the Government considered it appropriate to keep itself from connecting directly with the masses in the Kashmir Valley. Ostensibly to retain the Kashmiri people's confidence upon the democratic credibility of the Indian Union, the national level polity at the Centre, and in most instances even at the State levels, abstained from establishing the tradition of intimate politician-constituency relationships with the common man, as it is practiced in other States. Successive Union Governments thus kept distance from the grass-roots Kashmiri socio-political discourse, and staked faith in local Kashmiri leaders – from village to the Valley levels – for them to nurture the hoary civilisational bonding of Kashmir Valley citizens with the rest of Indian nation.

> ... the local 'leaders' found no inclination to seal the cognitive bondage of the people of Kashmir Valley with their Indian roots and its post-independence democratic dispensation. In fact "Indian Government" became a handy whipping boy for all ills – real, exaggerated or made up – that afflicted, or did not, the Kashmir Valley...

Keeping itself in the background thus, the national leadership promoted some bit leaders of societal, wealthy and religious backgrounds to act as intermediaries between the Indian Union and the Sate of J&K and so consolidate their hold over various groups and constituencies of the people of the

Kashmir Valley. Perhaps it was hoped that these leaders would use their influence to nurture the popular perception of Indian nationalism as it prevailed at that time, albeit with adequate autonomy for the Kashmiri people. In the event, these bit leaders amassed wealth, assumed tall standing, and to keep it that way, directly or in subtle manner, instigated an expedient practice of India bashing. That left the theme of State politics, grassroots upwards, to be marred by machinations to grab power, habitual biddings for the Union's largesse and unabashed graft of public grants. Obviously, economic uplift, indistrialisation, education, health and employment generation did not find priority in that scheme of things. All this while the Union Government either watched in passive interest, or worse, joined in chair-grabbing political chicanery of the favourites – favourites whose interest focused upon self-aggrandisement – at the cost of nationalistic consolidation, if that helped.

That Valley-based tussle for political control soon degenerated into propagation and counter-propagation of outlandish 'demands' to titillate populism and a licence to indulge in power manipulation and religious fundamentalism. Conversely, intermittent expression of angst became a standard ploy to garner more advantages – without accountability – from the Indian Union. As time went by, the game of crass opportunism, bargaining and brinkmanship emerged as the plank of relationship between the local manipulators – pretending 'leaders' actually – and the Kashmiri citizens with the Indian State.[5] The Union Government thus exposed itself to fatuous allegations over policy and practice 'deficits' in governance of the State, while leaving the local leaders free to promote their selfish agenda of power and wealth. More disturbingly, the local 'leaders' found no inclination to seal the cognitive bondage of the people of Kashmir Valley with their

Indian roots and its post-independence democratic dispensation. In fact "Indian Government" became a handy whipping boy for all ills – real, exaggerated or made up – that afflicted, or did not, the Kashmir Valley. Contrarily, having been 'purged', under threat of life, of its original 'Pandit' inhabitants, and most of their property 'transferred' under dubious deals, the Valley was practically turned into a 'Muslim Only' part of the State where, ironically, the majority enjoyed all the advantages granted by the Indian Union to all its minorities elsewhere in the country. That is so that over the past seven decades, the Kashmir Valley has been, in many ways, allowed to remain excluded from the national mainstream.

> ... some of the departures from Article 370 brought more power to people – like bringing J&K under the jurisdiction of the Supreme Court – were appreciated by the Kashmiris, but such advantages were left out of separatist discourse ...

Admittedly, there was popular support for application of the Article 370 of the Constitution which offered special judicial, economic and administrative provisions for the State. But for its wanton misuse, that exclusivity may neither be unusual nor undesirable – there are many similar provisions in the Indian administrative system. But when that exclusivity became a platform for gross abuse of nationhood on the one hand, and repudiation of promised autonomy and the trust that goes with it on the other, the matter required serious reconsideration. Herein, when it came to the basics of democratic and secular integration, the Government sponsored, and by now entrenched Kashmiri 'leaders' took to sabotaging those ideals. They took to blackmailing the Government with separatist calls, the purpose being to perpetuate their ransom of unbridled, unaccountable and money spinning overlordship.[6]

The Union Government responded, not by advocating with people and good governance, but by belying the visible signs of State autonomy that the people, as they believe, had been promised to them – use of nomenclature of 'prime minister' for the State, for example. That some of the departures from Article 370 brought more power to people – like bringing J&K under the jurisdiction of the Supreme Court – were appreciated by the Kashmiris, but such advantages were left out of separatist discourse.

Debase of Politics

Over the following decades, an environment of socio-political wrestling for special status, left unchecked under questionable pretexts of democracy and State autonomy, found vested interests among the people of the Kashmir Valley. Soon, in the competition for political power, democratic scruples were jettisoned and groups of 'collaborators' at the Union and State levels formed up to prepare their political bases for power-grab. Legislative bodies were subverted, State Governments were felled, elections manipulated, rabble rousing promoted and fiscal misappropriation ritualised thus. It was only time before these groups, backed by their wealthy patrons, both local and foreign based, found themselves as societal heavyweights.

> ... crass opportunism, bargaining and brinkmanship emerged as the plank of relationship between the ... pretending 'leaders' and the Kashmiri citizens with the Indian State ... call for democracy ... turned into demand for licence in the name of autonomy, corrupted into a rhetoric for *azadi*, and finally thrown up radicalised Wahabist venom ...

All this while, the national leadership did not, or was not allowed to, establish direct discourse with the people of the Valley, as it had been the practice in all other States and regions, thus leaving the field to the entrenched local leaders to have their 'field-day'. Over the years, India-bashing, while enjoying the congeniality of Indian Union, turned into a political lever. But as stated, even if many Kashmiri votaries started to contest their Indian identity while closely guarding the privileges of Indian citizenship, serious anti-nationalist activism did not appear before the closing years of the 1980s. Till then, there was little of the worrisome rise of anti-nationalist activism, packaged with Islamist radicalisation, in the Valley that became the norm afterwards.

> ... broadcast through radio, television and print media from ... Pakistan occupied areas, over the years played a key role in building up a adversarial narrative ... local mosques and Friday congregations were turned into factors of anti-national propagations ... Valley was thus consumed by a false narrative with clear cut assignment of roles: India 'the villain', Pakistan 'the saviour', fundamentalism 'the cause' ... all these years, the Indian broadcast was either missing or poor in content and reach; advise to attend to that vulnerability was ignored by the powers-that-be in New Delhi. ...

Notwithstanding the efforts applied, and some positive impressions made – successful elections and Kashmiri participation in political, professional and military mainstream, for example – it was clear by the later part of 1980s that in the overall context, the Indian Union's as well as the J&K State's policies on integration of Kashmir had failed to deliver. The situation offered an invitation to Pakistan, its power seeking agents in Kashmir and the fundamentalist among the Sunni clergy to inject *Wahabi* radicalism into the sublime tradition of Islam that had so far prevailed in the Kashmir Valley. Indeed, appealing, enticing and incessant propaganda of subtle as well as virulent kind, broadcast through radio, television and print media from the nearby Pakistan occupied areas, over the years played a key role in building up a adversarial narrative among the people of the Kashmir Valley. Similarly, loudspeakers of local mosques and Friday congregations were turned into factors of anti-national propagations. Lies, rumours, insinuations and falsifications about the Indian – read Hindu – governance, packaged with elements of observable facts thus had a field sway over a people already susceptible to misleading by co-religionist and co-ethnicities of Pakistan Occupied Kashmir (PoK). The Valley was thus consumed by a false narrative with clear cut assignment of roles: India 'the villain', Pakistan 'the saviour', fundamentalism 'the cause'. Notably, all these years, the Indian broadcast was either missing or poor in content and reach; advise to attend to that vulnerability was ignored by the powers-that-be in New Delhi.

The subterfuge of 'two-nation theory', targeted at the Indian Muslim, was reinforced by externally funded propagation of base religious fundamentalism. The Valley's traditionally accommodative Muslim society was infused with imported practices that were rooted at radical interpretations of the religion and its stricture-laden *takfiri* inquisitions. The rise of secessionist bigotry was intrinsic to that form of religious 'disorientation', so to say, of the tempestuous sections of the Kashmir society.

Thereafter, infiltration of Pakistan sponsored terrorists and coalescence of a partnership of secessionist militancy in the Kashmir Valley was but a foregone conclusion. Eventually, the agent provocateurs among that section were 'motivated' by the conglomerate of Pakistan State-Intelligence-Taliban combine to marshal – through religious indoctrination, monetary temptation and lure of political control – gangs of idle youngsters into pro-Pakistan, *azadi* (independence) seeking militant accomplishes.[7]

Enter Violent Secessionism

Given Pakistan's fundamental 'Islamist' pretensions and international nonchalance over its dubious activities, the situation turned vicious in the early-1990s. The Union Government's reticent, hands-off approach allowed Pakistan's radical Islamists to inject the ideology of religious extremism into an otherwise placid Muslim population in the Valley. Incessant brainwash led to the emergence of crops of home grown activists who could be used to harbour, support and assist hardened *Mujahideens* who had been rendered 'surplus' from the recently ended Afghan War, and who, in joining up to 'liberate' Kashmir from the 'clutches of the infidel', found a new purpose to their life. Thus in the garb of securing the "Kashmiri peoples' right of self determination" – a right actually trampled upon by Pakistan – a joint-venture of armed militancy cast its shadow over the once peaceful and placid Kashmir Valley. Soon enough, the subterfuge of 'self-determination' – 'proxy war', as it is described – exposed itself as a religiously sanctioned political and commercial venture for Pakistan's politician-Mullah sponsors. Similarly, in the Kashmir Valley, rabid manipulators joined hands with fundamentalist Mullahs and paid preachers to find profit from fanning turmoil in the Valley upon the shoulders of the youth who had been assiduously misguided by the call of 'religious duty' to join Pakistan. The enchantment of radicalisation, the bravado of raw gun-power and titillation of rebellious image drew groups of idlers to mob-provoking slogans and anti-national photo-shoots. Gradually over time, as the zeal amongst foreign 'guest' militants to 'liberate' fellow Muslims waned, young local romantics were saddled with the burden of *jehad* under the tutelage of the former. Along the way, the rhetoric for 'self-determination' had been exposed to be a matter of crass religious radicalism – a case of making of another 'Daesh' in the Kashmir Valley.

> ... the Valley was practically turned into a 'Muslim Only' part of the State ... in the garb of securing the "Kashmiri peoples' right of self determination" – a right actually trampled upon by Pakistan ... a joint-venture of armed militancy cast its shadow over the once peaceful and placid Kashmir Valley ...

All this while, besides deploying security forces to prevent, by minimal intervention, the secessionist forces from succeeding, there was little serious and substantive effort from the Union as well as the State Governments to deal with the rising romanticism of rebellion and its political and fiscal profitability. In contrast, Kashmiri leaders, rather than going to their people and engage with them, chose to seek security and comfort behind their richly constructed 'walls', thus leaving the field open for anti-nationals and religious bigots to intimidate, dictate and convert the people.

Conversely, anti-national calls from the secessionists and their interest groups – prompted under threat by Pakistani terror controllers as well as the self-invented ones – were responded with more distancing of the national political leadership and increased dependence on selected Kashmiri 'leaders' who pretended to be in control. Arguably, since the 1996 or so, there have been three occasions when the security forces had driven the militancy into near oblivion, but the disconcerted political establishments at the Union and State levels could not come together to convert these opportunities to secure lasting political stability and societal peace in the Valley. Continuation of anti-national armed uprising and its escalation to an unprecedented level was therefore only a matter of time.

Consolidation of False Narrative

During the past seven decades, various partisan narratives, each construed out of concoctions, insinuations, falsifications and blatant misrepresentations over the State of J&K's accession, the idea of plebiscite, democracy, human rights etc. have coloured the people's perceptions around the Kashmir 'problem'. The falsehood is so pervasive that most do not care to appreciate that the Indian offer of plebiscite in Kashmir was rendered un-implementable, and subsequently impossible, by Pakistan's refusal meet the first UN stipulation and vacate its aggression. Truly, the Pakistanis, Indians, locals of the Kashmir Valley, masquerading 'agents' of Islam, and global players who look to gain one way or the other from resolution or otherwise of this imbroglio – the Americans, high priests of Islam, the Chinese and possibly the Russians – all of them suffer from such clouded perceptions. The result is that pressurised, harried and sometimes cornered by diplomatic expediencies over a period, India has had to give ground by having to concede that Kashmir was an issue in 'dispute'. That allowed Pakistan and its Kashmiri hirelings to spread further misinformation regarding the 'Kashmir problem', while stage managing, by covert means, spectacles of anti-national activities in the Valley for brazen but sellable propaganda.

It is not that Pakistan's congenial duplicity is unknown to the world principals, but the disconcerting, if unstated, inference is that India's civil and military diplomacy has not been able to make its mark in rescuing the Indian Union's head-stuck policies on conclusive integration of Kashmir.

Fermentation of People's Estrangement

In the post-accession period, having used the Indian State first to save Kashmir from takeover by Pakistan and then to seek autonomy to the extent bordering at independence, the Valley-harvested anti-national forces have adopted three steps to derange the common man's loyalty to the Indian Union. The pattern, as described below, is noteworthy:

(a) Firstly, at the beginning, petty rabble-rousers of Kashmir Valley used the Congress Party to secure acceptance as the political representatives of all regions and different ethnicities of the entire State of J&K. Then, making suggestive use of religion to reinforce their grip over the Muslim majority population of the Kashmir Valley, they usurped the status of people's spokesmen, and so attempted to create their autonomous fiefdoms – 'emirates', so to say – in which they would reign and prosper while the Union bore the burden of economic sustenance, and maintaining internal stability and external security.

(b) Secondly, as the events leading to the clampdown in 1953 and the subsequent events up to the late 1980s signify, the intent appeared to be to sabotage the State's accession to the Indian Union. That attempt was foiled by the Indian Government. But in an unrequited offer of recompense, the Government bent backwards to promote some more opportunistic interest groups in the hope of balancing partisan loyalties. That led to encouragement of a culture of factional competition, base opportunism and blatant corruption in the Kashmir Valley, all perpetrated by the local political groupings, fundamentalist Grand Muftis' and their fanatic cohorts down the ladder. The rhetoric of separatism thus found vested interests among a constituency of political, religious and economic beneficiaries of State largesse and their unaccountability against corruption. But when self-aggrandisement came to question, even virulent competitors among these groups would join hands and turn mutually amenable, even pretending nationalist, the cause of true nationalism being the dispensable item.

(c) Finally, most such factions opted to shed their mask of *Kashmiriyat*, and declaring submission to crass treason in the pretext of Islamist consolidation, sought merger with Pakistan, 'self-determination' and 'separatism' being its euphuism. The lead instigation for that step came from religious radicalism among the Muslim majority – in just the Kashmir Valley, in the other two larger regions of the J&K, politics and religion retained their pristine distinction. Noticeably, the 'Pakistan' and 'Muslim' card now became but a trick to turn the State into an independent oligarchy. In that case, even if Pakistan would be mortified by its loss of 'Muslim territory', it would still find the satisfaction of breaking up India.

To that end, a handful of opportunists have waged sustained campaigns to estrange the Kashmiri people from the idea of India, and growing in influence over the decades have succeeded in alienating virtually the entire population of some six districts in the Valley. It is indeed the misfortune of the people of J&K that these districts have become a face of the majority 'will' in the entire State. Indeed, it is ironical that a *small pocket of Sunni Muslim predominant Kashmir Valley has fallen into the grips of rabid agents of secessionism*. By outnumbering the rest of the inhabitants of a many times larger but sparsely populated State, they seek to divert the eternal Indian destiny of all the citizens of J&K – Hindus, Buddhists, Shia and Sunni Muslims, Gujjars and Bakarwal Muslims and many others – all of whom dread the prospect of being the subjects of Pakistan or to live under the rule of a Taliban incarnate. Needless to reiterate, behind a false front of the clamour for *'azadi'* lurks the crass seduction of *Wahabi* extremism. The false front is exposed when these anti-national activists find it hard to spell out as to what the term *azadi* might imply to their future.

... population of some six districts ... have become a face of the majority 'will' ... to divert the eternal Indian destiny of all the citizens of J&K – Hindus, Buddhists, Shia and Sunni Muslims, Gujjars and Bakarwals, and many others – all of whom dread the prospect of being the subjects of Pakistan or to live under the rule of a Taliban incarnate ...

During the past two decades or so, the situation in the Kashmir Valley has grown even more vicious due to stranglehold of Islamist fanatics, who besides being anti-Muslim, anti-Kafir, anti-women and anti-freedom, have made common cause with Pakistan's ruling regime – 'deep state', as it is described. Today, all rungs of the Valley's Muslim religious hierarchy – mullas, maulanas, muftis, grand muftis, etc, – have turned rabid anti-nationals, while social, education and administrative institutions have succumbed to what is but a fatuous 'call of religion' to affiliate with Pakistan.[8] Likewise, the societal dons undertake to chorus, or made to do so under Pakistan based terrorists' allurement-and-threat, for separatism and merger with Pakistan. It is a situation when violent militancy is changing hands from infiltrated Pakistani terrorists to their local surrogates. Unchastised, even uncontested by nationalist institutions including the Indian State's civil apparatus itself, treason of a few has infected the Sunni Muslim masses of the Kashmir Valley – the infection is deepening by the day.[9]

In sum, the call for democracy in 1947 has been, over the following decades, hijacked to enrich political wheeler-dealers, turned into demand for licence in the name of autonomy, corrupted into a rhetoric for *azadi*, and finally thrown up radicalised Wahabist venom to kill the Indian nationhood.

This commentary would remain incomplete unless the alienation of the people of the Kashmir Valley is tested in light of many such instances in post-independence India, the purpose being to highlight the gravity of the Kashmir issue. The facts related to Kashmir Valley are:

(a) One, the overwhelming majority of the people of Kashmir Valley are inclined to offer their allegiance to Pakistan – the cry for *azadi* is a humbug, of course – *on account of their being Muslims;*

(b) Two, the Valley's vulnerability rises from its *contiguity to the Pakistan infected part* of Western Kashmir;

(c) Three, Pakistan's pretension of being the 'liberator' of all Muslims and its propensity to resort to unrestrained *use of overt and covert aggression* to justify that pretension would, in the foreseeable future, not allow it to let Kashmir be in peace;[10] and,

(d) Uncontested over the decades, an obsessively fabricated and incessantly injected narrative of India trampling upon their religious-political autonomy has been so deeply ingrained into the Kashmiri mind that it would take years of dedicated effort to cleanse that solidified mistrust.

These facts make the Valley a completely different case in comparison to say, Nagaland, Manipur or Assam. Then there is the clinching consideration: A 133 crore nation of numerous ethnic, religious and linguistic followings, all these but naturally fused into one nationhood, cannot let a part of its territory to be dissected by a misguided lot of just 69 lakh residents of just few districts who form but a small fraction of their 18 crore co-religionist – the proud Muslim citizens of the rest of the country. The secessionist notion is preposterous and an affront to civilised cognisance. Obviously therefore, the Vale of Kashmir requires an invigorated solution to retrieve it from the clutches of religious bigots, anti-nationals and traitors.

We may begin that quest with an overview of the current scene in the Kashmir Valley.

PART 2: THE PREVAILING SITUATION

The Locale of Secessionism

It is obvious that the fundamental principles of our nationhood have failed to find favour within a cognitively sequestered Kashmir Valley. Today, most among the 69 lakh people of six districts of the Kashmir Valley – out of the total population of 125 lakh from all the 22 districts of the State – would nod contemplating to an offer of secession from the Indian Union, howsoever impractical that idea they might actually know to be. A good percentage of young people among them are indoctrinated enough to adopt violent means to display their radical Islamist credentials and its construed corollary – secession from Indian Union. But with larger regions of the State – Jammu, Kashmir South of the Pir Panjal Ranges, and Ladakh regions – and the Muslim, Hindu and Buddhist population of these regions casting their destiny with the Indian nationhood, the secessionist demand, when shorn of subterfuge, sounds ludicrous.

Truly, even in that nursery of secessionism, the rabble rousers of Kashmir Valley turn uncertain as to what they might want 'after'. Clearly, that is a sign of the secessionist instigation being directed from an external source – Pakistan, of course. But some 19 crore Pakistanis and their localised agents of terror cannot be permitted to impound the ideals of 133 crore Indians, a sixth of the humanity spread over a sub-continent, who are dedicated to their sovereign, democratic and secular nation-state.

The Scene and the Players

An intense strife has engulfed Kashmir Valley from July to October of 2016. This strife is but a repeat of what took place in

Areas where anti-nationals have gained ground

2010-11, but more widespread, intense and prolonged. Predominant in six districts of Southern part of Kashmir Valley adjoining the PoK, and spilling over to another four districts, it gives an appearance of mass revolt against the constitutional State, triggered by a conglomerate of organised terrorists and militant secessionists instigated by the Pakistan State and its local agents respectively. Though the situation gave an appearance of having stabilised during the months of severe cold, actually there is no let up in flagrant defiance of the authority of the State and its law and order enforcement agencies. Observing the emboldened manner in which groups of masked and unmasked men provoke, mock, surround and assail the police and the State machinery, there does not seem to be an end to this tumult in sight.

The script is more or less repetitive. In larger villages and townships, young males, as if on a signal, come out of their homes after breakfast, and congregating at a prominent junction, proceed as one mob to prevent movement, ransack government property and attack security pickets. Besides being armed with as many stones they can carry and ensconcing the *agent provocateurs* amidst, they are trailed by cache of stones and brickbats of sizes collected to cause grievous injury. When restrained by the police columns sent out to keep control, they take to a well rehearsed sequence of stone pelting and advancing, as a surge of madness, towards the police. As police inch backwards to avoid physical clash, another group or two appear through by-lanes to hem them from all sides, which is like a pack of Hyenas nibbling at an entrapped animal. As the atmosphere turns into a frenzy, police tries to break up the mob by firing tear gas, rubber pellets and when situation goes beyond a point, even bullets. Then, just as one or two 'bodies' stumble injured, the mob is signalled to break up and run, individuals vanishing into by-lanes and homesteads. Within minutes, there is eerie silence in the stone strewn scene as policemen carry the injured 'protester(s)' to the hospital.

> ... innate characteristics remains moored to the hoary Kashmiri culture (*Kashmiriyat*) and a sublime Islam, even if in the toxic militant mind, educated or literate, that culture stand repudiated in favour of radical Wahabist impositions ...

For the next part, the scene shifts to public areas like bazaar, office areas and hospitals. Here, distraught relatives are joined by agitated 'friends' while scribes, probably under the *provocateur's* watch, to record the 'memorable' event through cell phone photography, 'WhatsApp' and media broadcast. Amidst much India-bashing, lamentations of police 'brutality', 'unprovoked' of course, plight of 'innocent' citizens, and 'frustrations' of psyched youth takes place. The satisfaction among the provocateurs of the 'movement' goes a few notches up should the injured 'innocent' dies; more the loss of life and pellet injury, more the opportunities for them. Meanwhile, a band of rather affluent Hurriyat leaders and their mufti-maulana minions, pepped up by anti-India penchant and guided by masters-financiers across the border, proceed to issue the next 'calendar' of protests and shut downs which would hopefully lead to another bout of well documented stone pelting, arson, firing, arson and death.[11]

Besides such occasions, the regular occupation of their paid agent provocateurs and maulvis who are trained in radical Muslim seminaries is to brainwash school children with hatred of 'Hindu India' and their purported 'responsibility towards extending the reach of Islam'. All this macabre Standard

Operating Procedure is quite in place to support the fabrication that 'all of Kashmir is in revolt' and 'freedom is being crushed under military boots'.

Forbidding Trends of Militancy

Described as expression of secessionist militancy, and with one late lamented smooth pretender as its poster-boy, the recent strife has many disconcerting scenes that had never been seen before at that scale. Besides the scene described above, there are ominous signs of escalating danger to India's national integrity, as exemplified by the following accounts:

(a) The proportion of local terrorists posing as 'commanders' or 'fighters' has increased substantially to vie with the number of Pakistani intruders; the ratio has now reversed to 70-30. These local 'rambos' are a savvy lot whose good living is sustained by government largesse and *Wahabi* terror funding from abroad. Most of these are attracted to Che Guevara kind of demeanour, albeit in form rather than in substance. Many youngsters glamorise these fellows though the parents are chary of their radical influence. *Rebelling for 'azadi', or merger with Muslim Pakistan is turning into a romantic pursuit.*

(b) There have been a chain of organised terror attacks on police stations and even few military campuses. Snatching of police weapons, arson of government property, ambush of ministers and sarpanches and intimidation of state functionaries have become frequent. The state-protected safe camp to accommodate Kashmiri Pundit employees was attacked so repeatedly that the occupants were left with no option but to flee, thus reversing the process of return of Kashmiri Pandits.

Indeed, the elaborate organisation and logistics behind these armed attacks, and *the reckless, even brazen, manner of execution of these continuously over time demands serious concern.*

(c) The anti-national theme which has been infused into the religious discourse, has now penetrated into the academic arena. While school children are taught to chant sedition, colleges and university students find it very enticing to flout themselves as India-baiters. India's supposed anti-Muslim, anti-Kashmir, anti-democratic afflictions and a plethora of mischievously invented, imagined and exaggerated ills have become the topic of campus talk. Absent, or at least hidden so far, disloyalty among the government employees is manifesting into collaborative involvements with the anti-nationals. *Brand of anti-nationalism has assumed credence.*

(d) Celebration of Pakistan's Independence Day and eulogy of 'Islamist' injunctions of the 'Daesh' variety have turned more exhibitionist. Sheltering terrorists and blocking security forces, even sloganeering and stone pelting to facilitate terrorists to escape capture are becoming a social practice. Militants' funerals are turning into mass events, though it is more in empathy with the local 'boys' families. Provocative brinkmanship like abusing, taunting and assaulting unsuspecting members of police forces, even in quiet conditions, is becoming an amusement prank among the younger lot. The underlying messages are the *vanishing fear of law, disdain of state institutions and peer adulation of anti-national behaviour.*

(e) Clearly stage-managed by agent provocateurs, even routine accidents, mishaps and losses are increasingly been ascribed to 'apathy' 'highhandedness', even 'ploys' of security forces, the outlandish propaganda is circulated to demand 'compensation'. Horror stories and morphed pictures, exaggerated beyond belief, are circulated and groups of protesters, with women in front, are herded to act out the farce of protests against anything and everything. Aided by a vernacular press that is motivated by its own safety, frivolous accusations are hurled, demonstrations organised and state property destroyed over a couple of days. Notably, curtains on the show are drawn before true facts are revealed, which in most cases point to deliberate fabrications and blatant lies. Most of t*he* Valley is shut down every fourth day, thus giving *impression of a genuine and popular freedom struggle, unless one is aware of the farce.*

(f) Human rights activists seem to have preferred their own safety against arbitrating in the strife. But compelled to find relevancy and funding, many of these have fallen to the expediency of outraging common sense by describing elimination of terrorists as "extra-judicial killing" and use of pellet guns as a "free pass".

More Ominous Indications

It is not that the entire mass or majority in the Kashmir Valley are crying out to merge into Pakistan or become an independent entity – comfort of being with Indian Union has not worn thin yet. But even then, it must be a matter of serious concern that even after seven decades of autonomy, progress and opportunities, visible estrangement with the Indian nationhood continues to be on the rise in the Kashmir Valley only to flare-out now and then. That is a warning bell to the approach of the danger-line against national integrity – this one needs to be heard. The ominous signs of that danger may be picked out from the following rather disturbing instances as seen during the recent inflammation of militancy :-

(a) Local courts, in deference to militants' sensitivities, are becoming liable to compromise on their compunctions against false charges, or even indicting security forces personnel on frivolous accusations. Government servants, who had so far saved themselves from it, are increasingly playing safe in displaying their anti-national affiliations and even acquiescing to do the militants' bid. Political functionaries have gone ambivalent in their public stance to preserve their existential future and yet avoid offending the militants. Agents of separatists are adulating those charged with sedition and trying to turn them into heroes. Militants are finding courage to attack the families of policemen. *The entire governing apparatus is being subverted thus.*

(b) The agitation had been so far confined more or less to five or six districts of Kashmir Valley adjoining the PoK. This time it spread to other four districts too. The ethnically diverse region of South of Pir Panjal Ranges and the Chenab Valley had earlier been affected only in exception. In a deliberate exercise this time, the organisers of militancy could push the agitation across that barrier. *Militancy seems to be spreading its area coverage.*

(c) Discredited except by their vested beneficiaries, the disjointed elements of 'Hurriyat Conference' have joined hands to gain relevance in the public discourse of the Valley. As agents of Pakistan's state and non-state Kashmir baiters, they are grabbing at the reins of the society through issuance of 'calendars' of shut downs, protests, funeral processions and boycotts. Point to note is that these pronouncements are no mere 'calls', but 'diktats' actually, overseen by agent provocateurs with hints of retribution – murder in the Valley is easy. *Separatists have thus found acceptance, if not following, among the masses.* Pompous in their confidence, they have gone ahead in proposing to some world leaders, some 'six steps' for the Indian Government to adopt – obviously to pave the way for them, as Pakistan's front-men, to reign over Kashmir, and smother dissent with radical Islamist whip.

> ... not that Pakistan's congenial duplicity is unknown to the world principals, but the disconcerting, if unstated, inference is that India's civil and military diplomacy has not been able to make its mark in rescuing the Indian Union's head-stuck policies on conclusive integration of Kashmir ...

There is a palpable apprehension that the above listed precursors may not be far from fruition – unless more effective measures, without succumbing to political, religious or motivated international pressure are adopted to restore the situation. Should a break-up become imminent and J&K turns into a war zone, none of the armchair 'conscience keepers' would be able to rescue the Indian nation from a societal explosion that would invariably follow.

A Feel of the Peoples' Pulse

There are official studies – as listed in Appendix A – which enumerate the causes that propel anti-national feelings in the Valley; these have to be taken note of in order to deal with the problem. Well known, these however would not be enough to remedy the peoples' estrangement. Interacting deeper, one finds that the situation in the Vale of Kashmir causes a mix of helpless resignation and despondency among its majority population. While the bands of separatists disorient them through pronouncements of disruptive and disloyal diktats, youngsters, mentored by foreign *jehadis*, are attracted to all forms of disorder to 'free Kashmir from the clutches of 'Hindu' India' (sic). Here, the Indian Union having really given no cause during the past seven decades for the Valley people to complain, indoctrination of young minds is packaged in two ways. One, even the State's innocuous and mundane administrative measures like legislation, minority welfare, management of education, sports, entertainment etc. are painted as infringements against Kashmir's – actually, the Valley based Sunni Muslims' – purported 'interests'. Call for agitation, unabashedly riding on religious intolerance, is then pronounced from separatist-religious pulpits, and hundreds of indoctrinated fanatics answer to that call in frenzied atmosphere. The second plank of secessionist indoctrination rests on ingraining a sense of deep fear among the young people with regards to what purportedly awaits their future. Herein, they are told that they have not adjudged India's true intent so far – that would emerge only after the agitating Kashmiris are silenced; whereupon a vengeful Hindu power would rush in to wipe out the Kashmiri Muslim identity. Thus indoctrinated with fear and violence to 'defend' their faith and way of life, there has *coalesced a sort of 'brotherhood' of young people coming from all social strata, who believe themselves to have been destined to wage war against the Indian Union.*

That leaves the middle and older age groups in a state of apprehension for the safety of their wards and loss of income from their trade. Truly, the common man is neither consumed by any partiality to India nor does he pine for Pakistan, he does not even relate to the call for 'azadi'. He wants peaceful life amongst basic amenities of modern times. His innate characteristics remains moored to the hoary Kashmiri culture (*Kashmiriyat*) and a sublime Islam, even if in the toxic militant mind, educated or literate, that culture stand repudiated in favour of radical Wahabist impositions. *The Indian State is vilified but Indians are not, the Army is respected but liked not, and the Indian State's amelioration of peoples' economic and natural difficulties is appreciated* but viewed as but 'entitlements' – being seen as a 'tax' for 'keeping' Kashmir. India, by her supposed 'arrogation' of Kashmir, is held equally responsible for triggering the scourge of militancy while there is much empathy with Pakistan's 'compellence' in having been left with no option – by India, of course – but to plunge into the surge of Islamist *jehad* against 'Hindu' rule over 'Muslim' Kashmir.

Notably, Pakistan's political intent as well as administrative capacity to give all the Kashmiri sects and ethnics a fair deal is widely suspected. The objective of agitation itself remains nebulous, and inconclusive. "Azadi we want", "Kashmir is not India, we are not Indians", "Our heart is in Muslim Pakistan", "we want tripartite talks to take place with Pakistan, India and the 'people of Kashmir' participating" etc. are the enticing slogans. More enquiries reveal that the agitators' ideas end here; there is no pretension regarding any possible manner to the materialisation of such hackneyed slogans or to reconciliation with the harder facts of geo-political implications thereof. It is also apparent, faintly of course, that the Government's largesse of subsidies and funds, stoic overlook of corruption and hands-off over anti-national pantomime have blinded the agitators from stark political and economic realities of separation. Similarly, the dangers of religion-sanctioned subservience, either by direct merger or by implication, to Pakistan are not fully appreciated, though the adult lot do display a sense of discomfiture and foreboding with that eventuality. Most concede that *Kashmir should not be Pakistan, nor would Kashmir, being situated next to Pakistan, be able to manage its independent existence.* Much discussion later, it is 'deniably implied' that the answer has to be found from the existing political system, somewhat in consonance with the Indian Constitution, that being the most agreeable course, the alternates being more agitation, societal bloodletting, radicalised religious barbarism, severe vitiation of regional politics, and finally, war. It is the misfortune of the common masses, as they themselves aver, that even if the agitation they acquiesce with comes to possible fruition, *break up from a democratic, secular and benevolent India would bring them greater and longer misery.*[12]

> ... some 19 crore Pakistanis and their localised agents of terror cannot be permitted to impound the ideals of 133 crore Indians, a sixth of the humanity spread over a sub-continent, who are dedicated to their sovereign, democratic and secular nation-state ...

But then, if that be the understanding of the stake-holding people of the Valley, what would the agitation be about? The answer to this query lies in the congruence of vested interests among three interest groups: One, Pakistan's aristocratic ruling class who need to project their '*ghazi*' (Islamic liberator) image to perpetuate their feudal status among their masses; two, non-entity mullahs who find power through radicalisation of Islamist injunctions; and three, the home grown hopefuls for power and pelf in the Kashmir Valley. This triumvirate of diverse agendas vie for autocratic power and unaccountable wealth, while corrupt propagations of a 'singular Muslim identity', ingrained over past three decades, resumes the Kashmiri Muslims' mind. It is also quite likely that the phenomenon of 'Muslim anguish' that emanates from external Islamist propaganda has found its own kind of manifestation in the spread of separatism in the Kashmir Valley.

Conceding to Harsh Realities

Without claiming absolutism of final verdict, deeper observations of the situation in the Kashmir Valley leads to the appreciation of certain realities. Quite well known, these realities are generally interned in the name of political correctness, preservation of local ethnicity, sensitivity of 'Muslim sentiments', fear of conflict exacerbation, adverse international opinion etc. Ironically though, all these ideals already stand mutilated by the secessionist militancy. In the process, the masses-at-large are abandoned to the manipulation of an autarchy of Pakistan sponsored Islamist agent provocateurs and some local anti-national hardliners-for-profit. Herein, it would be in order to elaborate the salient observations.

Secession has turned into a Muslim Issue. To begin with, the dispute over accession of the State of J&K was triggered by political ambitions with just an undertone of Muslim identity, the religious factor being played down in deference to 'political correctness'. Presently, that fig leaf over that political ambition, for secession from the Indian Union, stands fully discarded. By Pakistan's and its Islamist agents' deliberately crafted and relentlessly prosecuted campaign, the issue in the Kashmir Valley has been turned into a religious *fatwa*. Today, the ruling narrative in the Valley blares out to propagate that breaking away from the Indian Union is necessary to propagate the Kashmiris' Muslim identity – that is, even if India is home to the world's third largest population of proud Muslims. It has taken Pakistan and its agents decades – overlooked and uncontested by the Indian State – to spread this jaundiced notion; it will take more decades to cleanse that perception.

Pakistan would not relent. We are aware of the Pakistani elites' obsessive quest to destabilise India not only to prove their ideology of religious incompatibility and the 'two-nation theory', but in the process use this ideology to perpetuate their power-grip over the feudal Pakistani society. Indeed, having indoctrinated their generations with poisonous narratives, rulers of Pakistan have turned India bashing and 'fight for Kashmir' into a potent formulae to secure popular support and to be in power. On the other hand, India's reserved response to their irascible hostility has encouraged them to accelerate their anti-India ventures, while global principals, even if troubled, have looked the other way in deference to their own immediate concerns. Having thus outsmarted, with immunity, their ideological *bête noir* India, there is no reason for Pakistan's ruling class to let go of a prop that consolidates their power and pelf. Those who call the shots in Pakistan would therefore continue to find ways to keep instigating violence in Kashmir, find new issues of dispute and *inter alia* spread destabilisation all across India to maintain their grip over Pakistan's resources and its exchequer.

Pakistan cannot let go. There is no hope ever of easing of the indoctrinated hatred injected by the Pakistan State into its individual citizens and institutions. Emergence of a constituency of violent fanatics in Pakistan is a result of that macabre investment. Further, from being non-state collaborators in Pakistan State's war on India and Afghanistan, terrorist organisations have, over the recent years, consolidated into discrete power centres, the radicalised Islamists' savage devastation of the Muslim world bolstering their devilry. Sensible citizens of Pakistan stand mute and marginalised thus – just as the majority in the Kashmir Valley are obliged to submit to the secessionist agents. Consequently, the combined force of fanatic stimulus and terrorists' indoctrination would not allow the ruling elite and the society to ease back on Pakistan's destructive policies; its discontinuation would be perilous. Pakistan's prosecution of various forms of covert and overt war against India is therefore a permanent affair as far as one can see.

India's approach to the integration of Kashmir Valley stand belied. Ever since the accession of J&K, the Union Government has observed sublimate principles to bind the people of Valley Kashmir, bringing democracy and prosperity, even allowing them to establish their partisan oligarchy over the other regions of the State. In overdoing that bit, it has allowed local political atmosphere to drift endlessly into corruption and malpractices, much to the people's disillusionment. More seriously, in the name of religious and political freedom, the Government has overlooked the practice of raking up the issue of 'accession' as a handy rhetoric of local politics. It has also overlooked the deliberately panned and executed infusion of Islamist radicalism and anti-nationalism into the younger generation even if these are much in contrast to traditional Kashmiri values. In all these respects, it has staked on the Kashmiri leaders –who have little incentive in doing so – to rein in the subversive activities. It has committed security forces just enough to keep anti-national activities from succeeding, but little more. As stated, over three distinct periods since the 1990s when the security forces had succeeded in disabling the militancy, the Government, by laying bet on discredited local syndicates and Central observers, failed to convert those successes into lasting political arrangement. Instead, the polity engaged in argumentative debates on real or construed constitutional aberrations, political band-wagoning, functioning of security forces, local elections and manipulative messaging with political and extremist power-brokers – all but futile.

> ... three distinct periods ... when the security forces had succeeded in disabling the militancy, the Government, by laying bet on discredited local syndicates and Central observers, failed to convert those successes into lasting political arrangement ...

The combined result is that:

(a) Firstly, the Pakistan State, its agents of religious heinousness, and its 'friendly' instigators would not mend their ways against what they see in India as an alluringly soft pray, but who, by its resilience, even then poses danger to their assumption of unbridled power and wealth. Relentless hammering at the foundation of Indian nationhood till it falls incapacitated is therefore taken as a mission. *Pakistan would not let Kashmiri Muslims to live satisfied till they herd themselves into the Pakistani 'pound'.*

(b) Secondly, In the smaller confines of the Kashmir Valley, India's accommodative politics, economic prop-up and societal sanguinity has failed to bear fruit; it has in fact, in the seven decades, allowed the growth of many thorns into the Indian nationhood. Here, the Indian State has left space for local machinations and manipulations to keep brandishing the long concluded issue of the State's accession to the Union as a tool to wrest advantages, and in that process allowed the fringe anti-national elements to rise, consolidate and become the visible face of the silent peace loving masses. *That is but encouragement to fascism rooted at religious radicalism; it cannot be an example of democracy.*

(c) Thus a potentially explosive situation has been created, wherein *neither can the secessionist demand from just six Kashmir Valley districts be allowed to determine the fate of the rest of the J&K, nor can the anti-national activities in the Valley, situated contiguous to the PoK, be overlooked.*

The matter therefore deserves a relook, firstly, to discard short term acquiescence with local political machinations in favour of establishing direct connection with the Kashmiri people, and secondly, to elevate policing functions from just stalling the militancy to its eradication, root and stem. Tolerance of the intense tumult in Kashmir, ups and downs of which have already crossed the quarter century mark, has gone so far that the nation's sovereignty is under severe threat as it had been never before. With anti-Indian activities turning into a romantic occupation among the indoctrinated 'faithful', the question is how long would the infection be permitted to bleed; do we want the business of 'thousand cuts' to go on for another seventy years?

> ... ground level social and political interactions among the Valley based Kashmiris with rest of India have been minimal while religious hardliners have been left free to vitiate the Kashmiri brands of sublime Islam ...

Let us therefore wade, free from prejudices and hackneyed notions, into examining as to what options the Indian Union and the State of J&K might have to remedy this infection that festers endlessly upon our nationhood.

PART 3: OPTIONS, EXPERIMENTS AND ADAPTATIONS

Separation Breeds Separatism

A *de novo* measure of the Indian State's policies to integrate Kashmir Valley into the mainstream Union reveals that the State has foiled all attempts, made over many decades by Pakistan, its 'Islamist' collaborators and the local hopefuls of power-grab, to alienate the Valley through violent means. Indeed, the State has honed its tactics and procedures rather well to achieve that end with the least of political, social and economic disruption, bloodshed and destruction. Militarily, no doubt this has been a commendable achievement, and that is not lost on the international observers. Arguably, however, there are two glaring failures which may be ascribed to the Indian State. These are:

(a) In societal and political terms, seven decades is a long time to fail to make headway on integrating just a small patch of territory that the Kashmir Valley is – or even to fail in reversing the escalation in acts of anti-nationalism, local militancy and imported terrorism.

(b) The State's military measures to keep the external and internal secessionists from wresting the Valley out of the Indian Union has stagnated at purely reactionary level. It has failed to deter the inimical forces, both external and internal, from continuing their relentless assault on Indian sovereignty – and that with impunity.

The inference is that separation of Kashmir politics and its society from the national mainstream, even if on valid reasons, has actually sustained the notion of separatism – or more correctly, secession.

Precedence's of Policy Adaptations

Considering that it is high time to reverse the spread and escalation of militancy – and more disturbingly, the rise of local militants – in the Kashmir Valley, it would be necessary to examine certain major policy adaptations as well as the practical measures to invigorate the process of militancy eradication. There are over a thousand of secessionist movements flickering around the world. Most of these are congenital dreams which live on in the minds of bands of people in perpetuity, making occasional splashes now and then, but fail to make mark due to the concerned State's ministration of overall harmonious law, order and economic conditions – in some instances even harsh clampdown. Then there are some which continue to remain in active business of propagating separatism, taking recourse to social boycott, agitation, violence, and under favourable conditions, even armed confrontation with the State.

> ... India covets no one's territory, but remains stoic over the fact that her noble intent fails to impress either Pakistan or China who believe her to be in illegal occupation of theirs ...

A brief recount of various strategies adopted by the affected countries to deal with some of the major cases of neighbourhood aided militant separatism in the contemporary era may therefore be revealing. Though no two situations are alike, here there are some basic similarities and these lessons, when shorn of motivations and ideologies, and duly customised for our situation, might offer some insight into fresh policy adaptations for the Indian Union to end the separatist trend in Kashmir Valley. Cues could thus be taken from the instances mentioned herein to be customised into the list of our intended initiatives.

Spain: Basque Separatism. One of the oldest case of political estrangement is the two century old Basque separatism in Spain. Its recent revival into armed militancy, from sanctuaries located in neighbouring France, occurred in 1968. Against militants' intimidation of the people and hundreds of murders, concerted operations of the 'Guardia Civil' – a force like our Rashtriya Rifles but with better wherewithal, including intelligence capability – and with some help from French police and the CIA, this uprising was neutralised by 1992. Bit of complacency of the Government thereafter led to revival of the ETA (Euskadi Ta Askatasuna) militancy in 2001. The tactics adopted by the ETA had three prongs: One, violent demonstrations and intimidation of those who showed disinterest in terrorist group's secessionist thesis; two, acts of sabotage and low intensity urban terrorism; and three, major terrorist acts like murders and bombings. This time, a combination of concerted intelligence based operations, effective prosecution of militants, fair dispensation of democratic autonomy and international solidarity led to erosion of militant's support base. Going further, the Government not only targeted terror cells but also their connections with political parties, social organisations, business groups and media which had been instrumental in providing logistic and economic assistance, willingly or under duress, to terrorist activities. Meanwhile, information and communication technology, duly incorporated into regional commerce, was harnessed to engage the youth in economic opportunities. Thus by 2011, militancy was neutralised and separatist afflictions constructively diverted. However, wishful longing for independence remains in cognitive hibernation, though there is no hope of its materialisation – unless there comes an occasion in the distant future for drastic political reconstruction of the Spanish State.

Turkey: Kurdish Separatism. Economically discriminated and culturally alienated by the Government for nearly a century, the Kurdish people have been in armed rebellion off and on to shirk-off Turkish rule over their homeland in South East Turkey, even aspiring to include the adjoining areas of Kurdish Syria, Iraq and Iran in the making of their dream 'Kurdistan'. In late-1970s, the rebels adopted Mao Zedong's strategy of guerrilla war, and simultaneously attempted to gain wider support base through deliberate purge of various societal ills. Over the following decades, a strong motivational base and creation of an army (Peshmerga) of its own to engage in a combination of insurgency and conventional confrontations allowed the Kurdish nationalist movement to gain control over many areas, though these could not be held for long. Response from the Turkey State invariably come through hard and effective military operations, including imposition of martial law, and the results on ground always went in favour of the State. But with innate alienation continuing to simmer, such phases of Kurdish suppression left enough room for revival of the insurgency. In mid-2000s, having gained military control over disturbed areas and then having at long last realised that a purely military solution does not work, the Turkish State succeeded in assuaging Kurdish masses through the institution of many beneficial policies on economy, education and employment. Peace and stability talks between rebellious leaders and the State become a regular affair thereafter, and it helped that Kurdish regions saw better administration. Though the secessionist hope has again been strengthened as a consequence of the decade long turmoil in Iraq and Syria, and the Peshmerga has organised itself with better training and equipment, the secessionist movement still remains clammed-up by each of the affected nations of Turkey, Syria, Iraq and Iran. Notably, international opinion does not come out in favour of according territorial status to 'Kurdistan', not by violence in any case. Turkey and Iran are powerful nations and international players are not ready to invite trouble by angering these powers.

Neo-Russian Secessionism. The Chechen Muslim rebellion against Russian rule has seen many ups and downs. Finally, its post-break up weakened Russian army was reorganised to hard-fight the insurgency to the ground. That purpose was achieved by force applied ruthlessly and unapologetically, and unmindful of the loss of life and destruction of entire townships. Conversely, there is also the Russia's case of 'reverse justification'. Taking advantage of its ethnic settlements, Russia used the extra-territorial loyalty of Neo-Russian majority in Eastern Ukraine and Crimea to annex the Crimean peninsula through well orchestrated covert and overt military operations. Notably, the Western powers have fiercely opposed the popular endorsement of Russia's overturning the sanctity of Ukraine's sovereignty. Geo-political machinations among the Western power group to chastise Russia goes on – may be the last of this episode is yet to unfold.

China: Tibetan Independence. China's ruling regimes have consistently sought to secure their territorial integrity by 'sinicising' the demography of its peripheral regions. Thus over the centuries, that policy has led to creation of Neo-Han ethnicities in faraway lands. The result is that China today is more ethnically and culturally connected than ever before. Tibet and Xinjiang Autonomous Regions, as indeed the other three autonomous regions, are contemporary examples of this connection. Here, China has opted to impose a combination of hard Sino-centric administration and measured doses of economic progress to keep the native people in 'distressed reconciliation' with Chinese rule. Meanwhile, long term scheme to alter the demography and bring about Han domination over native ethnics continues briskly. Applied resolutely in firm dismissal of international and local consternation, this policy will merge these regions into the Chinese mainstream a few decades down the line, economic benefits playing a catalytic role in that assimilation.

Pakistan: Religious Separatism. Pakistan was created by invocation of exclusive Muslim identity. Even if that idea failed to move the majority of Muslims of undivided India, and scotch separatist sentiments among the Bengalis, Balochs and Pushtuns, Pakistan's urge to capture Kashmir remains untamed. Meanwhile, Pakistan encourages Sunni Punjabi business and trade based migration into the PoK. It also construes fundamentalist religious injunctions to negate the pulls of disparate sects and clans among the Muslims and so to secure its integrity as an Islamic nation. Here, the idea of Islam, as interpreted by 'approved' schools of Wahabi injunctions are hopefully used as the assimilating force.

> ... notwithstanding our self-congratulatory propagations, Pakistan remains neither censored nor isolated ... China's increasing control over the PoK could be a harbinger of Sino-Pakistan joint venture to capture the rest of the Indian State of J&K on some pretext or the other ...

The inferences are clear. In most cases:

(a) The way to healthy nationalism is better paved by the offer of regulated political autonomy, free social interaction, religious harmony and economic dependencies.

(b) Within these parameters, however, the fact remains that to prevent the rise of intractable political estrangements and secessionist activities, permanent solution have come only through hard enforcement of internal order, fair and firm administration and demographic balancing over a period.

(c) Astute management of information to foster factual and positive understandings – 'nationalist indoctrination' to put it starkly – through a credible information machinery is key to the repudiation of separatist affliction among the people. US and China, among many others, pay much attention to infuse nationalist spirit among their young citizens, so do we, but somehow that thrust peters out before it reaches the Valley.

In the smaller confines of Kashmir Valley, serious application of the aforementioned conditions have been withheld so far in a hopeful subscription to democratic and autonomous administration. The Union Government's limiting its responsibility just to the maintenance of economic stability and societal order and near-abdication of administration to local power-brokers have allowed the Valley sentiments to reverse from its post-accession endorsement. This apart, ground level social and political interactions among the Valley-based Kashmiris with rest of India have been minimal while religious hardliners have been left free to vitiate the Kashmiri brands of sublime Islam. In similar vein, conditions for economic and industrial uplift have been left to the rather unenthused national entrepreneurship. Failure of this policy of 'hands-off' reticence in the Kashmir Valley, even if that made no headway after seven decades of its continuation, does not leave any doubt about perpetuation of endless cycles of violence and agitation in the foreseeable future. Indeed, end of mayhem in Kashmir requires new policy adaptations, experimentations, fine tuning and implementation – resolutely and by discard of prejudices, trepidation or stale clichés.

Factors that Invigorate Pakistan

We have discussed the then Indian Government's innocent belief over fair arbitration of the Kashmir issue at the UN. But alas, international politics goes by law and logic only till broad consensus prevails – contentious matters are decided but by force. This reality is most evident in matters of territorial disputes wherein application of force in various forms plays decisive role – that is how it has been and so will it ever be. But even then, there are two factors which influence the course of territorial disputes, and those encourage Pakistan to be optimistic in its Kashmir venture. These factors are:-

(a) One, in modern times of people's empowerment, majority endorsement, if not submission, to the authority of the State they live in, is a condition needed for permanent territorial stability.

(b) Two, bereft of majority support over the periods of decades and centuries, anti-state rebellion rides through cycles of strength and weakness till finally the territories turn liable to transfer of sovereignty.

(c) Success of secessionist movements is bolstered by a supportive neighbour.

Pakistan has found it expedient to turn Kashmir into a 'core issue' of her existence as a nation and a plank to secure domestic political power. Enchanted by the favour of the above mentioned two factors, Pakistan is sanguine that its capture of Kashmir, if not the entire State of J&K, is imminent, just a push away. Thus consumed by an innate propensity to use force to have its way while stoking estrangement among the people of the Kashmir Valley, Pakistan remains encouraged to wage its relentless assault to wrest the part of the State of J&K that remains in India's control. Having described Kashmir as its 'jugular vein',

Pakistan's existence as a nation-state is inexorably tied to capture of Kashmir and therefore, Pakistan cannot give up its stake. No doubt, the Kashmir issue would remain in contention, unless of course that recalcitrant usurper is left in no position to usurp.

> ... Kashmiris' new found fundamentalist Islamic injunctions against non-Muslim governance would not permit them to live satiated in secular India – unless their loyalty is secured with economic progress and infrastructural uplift ...

With the spread of organised stone pelting, growing crowds in *janaja* (terrorists' funeral) processions and rising incidents of mobs coming out to shield terrorists trapped by the security forces, both the above mentioned factors have started playing against the Indian interests. That invigorates Pakistan. Wisdom states that it is time for India to give a fresh impetus to the treatment of this epidemic at its root and symptoms before another opportunity to get to the grips of the situation goes by.

Our Perfunctory Notions

Given to professing peaceful intent, non-violence, responsible international conduct etc., India expects her sovereignty to be respected by her two inveterate antagonists. But she plays down their gross violations of her integrity by the fuelling of internal disturbances, arming and incitement of neighbours and barter of her territories usurped. India covets no one's territory, but remains stoic over the fact that her noble intent fails to impress either Pakistan or China who believe her to be in illegal occupation of theirs. In contrast to such adversarial challenges, we are liable to find solace from exaggerated notions of India's defence capabilities that exceed the actual level of preparedness, howsoever laudable these may be. Thus just as in considering the possession of a large military force, its debilitating 'hollowness' is glossed over, and missile tests are flaunted to count for conventional hard power, in similar vein, elections in J&K are viewed as endorsement of the State's accession, saboteurs and traitors are humoured as 'misguided innocents' and small scale 'surgical strikes' are celebrated as profound 'victory'. 'Feel good' seems to be an enchanting banality among us and our leaders.

> .... mature democratic governments adapting to extraordinary measures in the interest of national integrity ... time to accept that only drastic quantum of soft-and-assuaging civil measures, reinforced with hard-and-disarming military action, over a period of time, would remedy the situation ..

In similar vein, we are liable to play down Pakistan's capacity to undermine India. Pakistan is seen as an undemocratic, underdeveloped, conceited and an irresponsible State, something which Pakistan is apparently not. Indeed, fewer of Pakistani citizens remain agitated against the Pakistan State and its feudal system, better fed and clothed they reportedly are, taming of Pakistan's recalcitrant frontier tribes is nearly complete, Punjabi Sunni flag bearers have been spread to all its corners and Pakistani leaders have winking camaraderie with most of the powerful world. Truly, Pakistan's nonchalant falsifications of the UN Resolution on Kashmir, suppression of Baloch and Sind nationalism, feudal exploitation of its peasantry, gender injustice, persecution of minorities, subscription to terrorism, religious vitiation of neighbourhood societies etc. seem to make little mark on the international conscience. Conversely, Pakistan's absurd claims over purported 'fight' against terrorism, and the farce of promoting cultural pluralism, minority interests and human rights, laughable as these would be but for the dangers the falsehood of such claims pose, seem to be lapped up by the world's principals. Doubtlessly, notwithstanding our self-congratulatory propagations, Pakistan remains neither censored nor isolated.

As for India's Chinese detractors, we humour ourselves with our 'bold face-offs' against Chinese Army encroachments astride the Line of Actual Control (LAC) while having to remain stoic against being hemmed-in from the North and West, and in the process of being encircled from the South too. Meanwhile, China's increasing control over the PoK could be a harbinger of Sino-Pakistan joint venture to capture the rest of the Indian State of J&K on some pretext or the other. Ironically, thus troubled by nations who are impelled by animosity against her, India still affords to revel in strategic stupor. Concessions made repeatedly over the decades for the benefit of the people of the Kashmir Valley without reciprocal appreciation of the idea of India could be a manifestation of that stupor. Meanwhile, the Americans have recently gone to the extent of eulogising Pakistan's war on Taliban heavens in North Waziristan and its purported disavowal of the Haqqani militants, while China's requited love for her selectively terrorist sidekick keeps growing. With China, United States and now Russia thus vying to pat its back, Pakistan's score over it five to seven times stronger 'rival', India, seems to be overwhelming. Thus while we Indians demonise Pakistan among ourselves, our genuine consternation fails to stir global conscience. No doubt that Pakistan is able to sell its 'Kashmir' cause better. No doubt that even if a pigmy it is, its satanic capacity to infect peace and stability needs to be neutralised.

> ... hard fact is that the Kashmir dispute cannot be reconciled – unless there occurs a geo-political restructure of the region ... enjoin us to first set our house in order and do everything that can possibly be done to ... deny the ground for Pakistan to play mischief ....
>
> ... there looms, more than ever, the signs of long tumult in the Kashmir Valley, and with it, the Islamist radicals plying their trade in the rest of India ...

We are well past the latest time to treat this subversive cancer – what we generously describe as 'separatism' but actually are acts of brazen treason. That the Indian State has allowed the situation to deteriorate so much and so deep, is a matter of serious introspection. The farce that goes on in the name of solidarity with so termed 'aspirations' and 'pains' of Kashmiri youth, criticism of the Union's supposed 'highhandedness', demand for recall of the 'Armed Forces Special Powers Act', condemnation of the 'demonic' use of the pellet gun, and such subterfuge may be permitted to be played out, but it is also the time to accept that only drastic quantum of soft-and-assuaging civil measures, reinforced with hard-and-disarming military action, over a period of time, would remedy the situation.

India's Advantages and Dangers in Kashmir

Fundamental to India's advantage in Kashmir Valley are four factors, each of these diverse in content but congruent in purpose. These factors are:

(a) One, India offers an accommodative democracy and unqualified freedom to its citizens, and that is an appealing antidote to the poison of radical separatism.

(b) Two, the thoroughly corrupt and unscrupulous agents of anti-nationalist agitation in Kashmir Valley and their murderous mad-caps are disqualified from emulating the ideology of any freedom movement. No nation has ever been 'liberated' by acts of terrorism.

(c) Three, the secessionist idea covers just a minuscule part of the State; it lacks the 'critical mass' to dictate its terms to the rest of the State and the nation.

(d) Four, in three occasions in the past, it has been possible for the security forces to nail the militancy to the ground. In these instances, the success could not be sealed by due political process due to the aforementioned practice of allowing local political motivations to distract the purpose. Suppression of militancy with resolute action is therefore well within India's capability.

(e) Five, the Indian's resilient nationalism, served by a war-worthy and idealist military, would not let the country break-up – unless it is internally undermined by treacherous machinations.

> ... Indian leadership to purge themselves of the trepidation of Kashmiri backlash, Pakistan's aggression, international reaction and arbitrary trial by some among the liberal community. All of these are already doing what maximum they could to undermine the Indian nationhood – there is little scope left for them to hurt India more ...

However, notwithstanding the advantages India possesses, harmony may still remain absent in the Kashmir Valley. Herein a small part of J&K, majority opinion against India's purported 'Hindu rule' remains flamed by Pakistan even after a rather lengthy period of seven decades. Even the sublimate nature of the Indian dispensation is unlikely to convert those who have taken to anti-nationalistic fervour in their radical interpretation of religion. Rather, aided by fugitive *jehadis* from elsewhere, the intensity of estrangement might turn even more expressive through scaled up violence. In the process, should popular exasperation with the situation goes beyond its already stretched limits, it would then be very difficult for India to retrieve its position.

As the aforementioned warning bells toll, there is little doubt that there looms, more than ever, the signs of long tumult in the Kashmir Valley, and with it, the Islamist radicals plying their trade in the rest of India. Doubtlessly therefore, the Indian State's authority needs to be enforced; the rhetoric of "winning hearts and minds" cannot be the sole recourse to curb disloyalty and treason. Indeed, it is time to shed our post-1990s phenomenon of political trepidation of strong measures, and adapt to new strategies to dismantle, once for all, the virus that festers anti-national infection. We may take cue from the precedence's of mature democratic governments adapting to extraordinary measures in the interest of national integrity – some of which have been discussed above.

> ... no insurgency may have been solved purely through application of force alone; but neither have any been solved without hard military action ...

Coming to Terms with Reality

Notwithstanding many well intentioned attempts made by Indian, Pakistani and world leaders, the Kashmir issue, when shorn of platitudes, insinuations, aspirations and real-politics, comes clear as an irretrievable problem for the foreseeable future. The dispute here is about:

(a) One, India's indelible territorial sovereignty over a Princely State that had legally, and by norms accepted at the time by leaders on either side as well as the people's representatives, acceded to the Indian Union.[13]

(b) Two, The ideology of Muslim exclusivity that led to India's partition and Pakistan's birth, and by implication, its life-line stake over a Muslim majority Kashmir. This claim has turned into a justification for Pakistan's nationhood.[14]

(c) Three, Kashmiri people's social estrangement with rest of India, Kashmiri politician's dream of independent rulership and Kashmir's wealthy and influential religious figures' urge to preside over the Kashmiri life.

Under this situation which of the contenders would dare to concede without inviting peril? The compelling conflict between the divergent positions is further cemented by a combination of geographical contiguity, religious affiliation and filial connections between India's Kashmir and its western part on the other side of the line of divide that, behind a facade of 'independent' status, stands occupied and ruled by Pakistan. Add to that the consternation among the Indian Kashmiris which decades of our defocused governance has allowed to replace their early admiration of the idea of independent India. Indeed, Kashmiri leaders, having failed in their perfidy of using India to deflect Pakistan's overtures and replacing monarchy with their own autarky, feel that India has retracted from the promises it made.[15] Ironically, even if Nehru's offer of plebiscite was spurned by Jinnah-Liaquat Ali in 1947, and the UN mandated plebiscite was derailed by Pakistan's refusal to comply with the first step of withdrawing from the entire State of J&K in 1949, it is India who is called upon to bear the onus.[16]

> ... engagement of all-India political, administrative, religious, educational and societal representatives ... particularly the youth, would instil among them the right confidence over the Indian system and promote the attraction of the sublime 'idea of India' that brings political, economic and religious freedom with it ... 'barefoot' mentors and counsellors can be drafted to ... play a key role in de-radicalisation ...

Further, the Kashmiris' new found fundamentalist Islamic injunctions against non-Muslim governance would not permit them to live satiated in secular India – unless their loyalty is secured with economic progress and infrastructural uplift. But such developments cannot grow in an area which is kept on the broil through the proxy war which is persecuted by Pakistan and further fanned by religious radicalism on either side of the Line of Control. The complexity reaches its peak when Pakistan applies its 'Muslim majority' factor to claim the Buddhist Ladakh and Hindu Jammu regions, whereas the citizens of these regions are petrified by the prospects of having to live in Pakistan.[17]

In sum, the hard fact is that the Kashmir dispute cannot be reconciled – unless there occurs a geo-political restructure of the region. Such reconstructions take decades if not centuries to materialise. These are the conditions that enjoin us to first set our house in order and do everything that can possibly be done to bring stability and prosperity in the part of Kashmir Valley where the Indian Constitution reigns – and so deny the ground for Pakistan to play mischief.

> ... anti-nationals among college students and petty trading community, the savvy and therefore more dangerous lot, have to be purged in order to save their peers from being infected by radical provocations ...

Options and Experimentations

At the outset, it must be appreciated that many substantial measures have been instituted by the Government of India, as well as the State Government, to ameliorate peoples' problems and assuage their angst against the Indian Union. These include skill enhancement, employment, education and livelihood schemes like UDAAN, USTAAD, Nai Manzil, reservation in educational institutions across India, cross LoC trade, etc. There is also the talk of applying classical 'solutions' like revocation of the Armed Forces Special Powers Act (AFSPA), release of 'political prisoners', inquiry into killings, result-oriented dialogue, economic uplift, protection of civil liberties and human rights, public awareness and involvement ... the list is long. Even if these 'solutions' are verbose and of limited practicality under the current situation, these should be acted upon. However, to make a difference in this extraordinary situation, the State has to break extraordinary grounds and devote to effective implementation of new provisions.

The first step in that endeavour would be for the Indian leadership to purge themselves of the trepidation of Kashmiri backlash, Pakistan's aggression, international reaction and arbitrary trial by some among the liberal community. All of these are already doing what maximum they could to undermine the Indian nationhood – there is little scope left for them to hurt India more. As seen from Basque, Kurdish, Neo-Russian and Tibetan examples, irrespective of the sanctity or otherwise of the cause, the world really cares little about such cases. In any case, preventing disintegration of the nationhood and all that it stands for needs no endorsement. No doubt, distraction from the noble cause to go overboard in acts of callousness and insensitivity have to be firmly repudiated – the common citizen must not be tormented. With a commendable record in that aspect, the Indian State need not be concerned on that account.

> ... any number of studies, experiments, fact-findings and recommendations ... remain unimplemented due to indiscipline in the State apparatus, diversion of effort by acquiescence with impractical democratic pretentions, and the tumult of militancy ...

No insurgency may have been solved purely through application of force alone; but neither have any been solved without hard military action. Settlement of the Irish secessionism, necessitated by the Irish Republic Army's inability to beat down the State, is an example. Time is ripe to let our security forces regain the near-complete subjugation of militancy as it had done before. Much of that condition already exists, but to make it conducive to successful completion, the security forces may be allowed to shift gear from reactive to pro-active mode. To achieve that end, Unified Headquarters may have to be militarised – as had been the practice in the 1960s, 70s and even 80s – and 'surge' resources allocated to the purpose. Military commanders have to raise the level of operations while exercising close control through unit and sub-unit commanders in the field, in strict adherence to the usual military honour code, so as to avoid undue overbearing among the troops and rise of angst amongst the people. Forces' casualties as well as collateral damages would have to be expected till the growth of secessionism is conclusively reversed. People of Kashmir Valley would have to be closely and routinely interacted with to propagate the State's sovereign but detested compulsions in adopting hard measures; reasonable words do have tremendous powers to blunt, to much extent, one sided anti-state insinuations, propaganda and incitements, and the popular sulk these generate.

The steel frame of State apparatus has to be de-rusted and vitalised. Judiciary has to be freed from fear of physical harm and the process of justice speeded up by providing higher security, posting of judges and staff from other States, opening special courts and raising the accountability of the prosecution. Similarly, to scotch the recently witnessed impropriety among the State employees, implicit and demonstrative loyalty must be demanded of them, and the handy excuse of 'militant threat' to their life to justify official apathy rejected. Here there is also a case for inter-state cross-transfer and cross-recruitment of State employees, which would also lead to employment generation, that arguably being the single cause of youth angst. No doubt, for their anti-national criminalities, lawful prosecution have to be pressed against terrorists, agent provocateurs, affluent power-brokers, corrupt public servants and radical muftis and maulvis– all of them the beneficiaries of political tumult and bigotry – by shedding the usual trepidation of instigated show of mob breast-beatings.

The State's dissemination of truth and balanced descriptions of events to the people-at-large leaves much to be desired. The field is thus left for insinuations, falsifications, incitements and cognitive vitiation. In today's environment of information awareness, that is a major cause of concern. We need to appreciate that the forces' occasional bonhomie during Eid, medical camps, school activities etc. are not enough to protect the people from daily doses of inflammatory subterfuge and religious incitements that the agents of separatism, particularly the ones among their own, inflict. A hard look at this weakness indicates that it is not a case of the State's deliberate reticence or dearth of themes, but a profound alacrity-deficit among the policy makers and lack of expertise at their disposal. This weakness at the State as well as Union level has to be overcome if the Kashmiris are to be better informed to see what is to their own good. Simultaneously, paid agents' provocative propaganda and crafty subterfuge would have to be countered by reason and demonstration of noble intent. Alongside, intimate engagement of all-India political, administrative, religious, educational and societal representatives with the Kashmiri people, particularly the youth, would instil among them the right confidence over the Indian system and promote the attraction of the sublime 'idea of India' that brings political, economic and religious freedom with it.

Our military-sponsored 'Sadvavana' (Goodwill) Scheme is arguably the most successful effort in earning the Kashmiri's faith. This Scheme however succeeds just because it is implemented through the military system, and is therefore free from petty politics, bickering of vested interests, administrative laze and corruption. While it would be too much to expect the military system to spread this Scheme to cover all aspects of civil life, there are many methods of achieving that end, as indeed it has been done many times before in India and abroad. The Army's 'Sadvavna' programme has to be translated at the State level, to be run according to its characteristic commitment and efficiency. Veteran servicemen would be better marshalled to serve that purpose.

The steps listed above would establish conditions for genuine political party functionaries to engage in grass-roots dialogue with people, youngsters, parents and community elders. 'Barefoot' mentors and counsellors can be drafted to engage in public discourse on social, political, educational, career, and such societal fundamentals, and so play a key role in de-radicalisation. Secularism need not prevent us from invocation of the pristine tenets of Islam to strengthen nationalism; Muslim counsellors, educators and religious teachers from other parts of India could play a significant role in this effort. At the beginning, the initiative would be fraught with logistic difficulties and physical risks, but it would be worth the cost and effort in saving the nation from living in a quagmire for unending decades.

> ... time therefore to devise new methods ... of timely and effective governance in the State. No doubt, vested interests might view such methods as undemocratic, and that such initiatives might invite a cacophony of alarm, but extraordinary times call for extraordinary measures ...

Madrassa education needs to be modernised and teachers as well as religious preachers – many of them coming from seminaries of Ahle Hadith, Tablighi Jamaat and Deoband – saved from *takfiri* intimidation and inducements to the parroting of anti-national sermons. More importantly, anti-nationals among college students and petty trading community, the savvy and therefore more dangerous lot, have to be purged in order to save their peers from being infected by radical provocations. Morphed images and false stories of 'suffering of Muslims' and 'rewards' of jihadist barbarism have to be publicly exposed – and punished.

One major deficit in the State's function in the Kashmir Valley is the scarcity of good governance. Given the seven decades of licence to indulge, bad, partisan and corrupt governance has taken deep roots in the system – a system manned almost in totality by local employees who are tied to their vested interests. Drastic measures would need to be instituted to undo that aberration. There are any number of studies, experiments, fact-findings and recommendations aimed at ameliorating the

Kashmiri angst. But these remain unimplemented due to indiscipline in the State apparatus, diversion of effort by acquiescence with impractical democratic pretensions, and the tumult of militancy. It is so that development remains frozen, unemployed youth sulk and militancy thrives to complete the circuit. It would need disciplined governance over a decade or two to break that circuit, when small steps would coalesce to produce the required surge of progress.

Under the native conditions, corruption free and benevolent governance, besides clampdown over anti-national activities, to be achieved within a short period, would need deliberate adaption of forceful, even strict, civil administration. Administrators have to be made to exercise full powers on implementation of various programmes and schemes, and to punish recalcitrance – with due redress mechanism to prevent aberrations, of course. Such forceful steps to retrieve the Valley from its vitiated situation – many of which might not be in the best examples of democracy – would have to be explained to domestic and global observers; the Indian State also needs to take all its people along in justifying expenditures and exactions that it needs to adopt to end the bottomless bloodbath.

Customised System of Governance

Considering the approach of an emergency situation in the Valley, it would be prudent to accept that the current idealistic system of party rule – with some interludes of Governor's rule now and then – has not worked in the State of J&K. It is time therefore to devise new methods – albeit temporary till the situation of revolt is mended – of timely and effective governance in the State. No doubt, vested interests might view such methods as undemocratic, and that such initiatives might invite a cacophony of alarm, but extraordinary times call for extraordinary measures.

> ... this is not the time to impose administrative or judicial strictures upon the security forces' options in dealing with fanatically charged anti-nationals ...

Cognition needs to be taken of the fact that presently, it is not democracy, but rabid fascism that prevails in the Kashmir Valley. Assumption of firm control over the State administration therefore, to foster stability, encourage nationalist politics and bring economic progress, may be considered by making provisions for adoption of extraordinary options, when necessary, in favour of nationalist interests.[18] These measures could be:

(a) It is very important to keep the State apparatus committed to the national cause. That needs a revamp of the system of validation of members of the legislature, ministers, judicial officials and government employees. Persons of doubtful nationalist fervour may be put through a legal process of scrutiny and offered voluntary retirement. The recruitment process should be streamlined accordingly. Cross-posting of employees, particularly new recruits, to other States may be thought of.

(b) The traditionally diffused authority to manage the State may have to give way to relative concentration as well as accountability for exercise of administrative power. The State's ministerial and administrative authorities should be empowered with simpler provisions for the exercise of administrative powers – like strengthening the provisions for promulgation of ordnances, executive orders, disciplinary and welfare issues and fiscal allocations. Provision be made for them to 'freeze' for a time, those contentious legal or procedural issues which defy resolution without being held to ransom by rabble-rousing factions. The 'majesty of the State' may thus be restituted to promote 'good governance' in the service of the people. Firm authority would also clampdown spread of poisonous insinuations, false stories and save the State from the 'Pandit and ex-servicemen colonies' kind of embarrassment – and the encouragement that gave to the rumbustious separatists.

(c) Reorganisation of Panchayat, Tehsil, Block and District Councils as partly elected and partly State sponsored bodies should be thought of. The system of instituting 'Governing Councils' of respected locals and proven administrators, for them to exercise larger administrative and fiscal powers at each level without being dictated by partisan manipulators, may be considered. Construction of schools, roads etc. would then not be held up to ransom by militants, religious radicals and their financiers, nor would the common citizen have to run from pillar to post to get what must be a matter of his right.

(d) Establishment of special fast track courts within and outside the State to expeditiously deal with anti-national cases. Law enforcement should be quick and visible.

The nation's exalted judiciary at the highest level has been active in its dispensation of benevolent justice to the victims of Kashmir mayhem. That is but an imperative for the people to have confidence in the majesty of our judicial system. However, it also needs to be appreciated that this is not the time to impose administrative or judicial strictures upon the security forces' options in dealing with fanatically charged anti-nationals who are bound by no scruples. It is a war-like situation and security forces are there at the nation's call; their tactical conduct cannot be put to scrutiny at hindsight based on concocted rhetoric. Orders, passed from safe distances, on filing cases against forces personnel, use of mob control measures (pellet guns, etc), institution of enquiries, etc., turn up as the anti-national's weapons and breed scepticism among the last bastion of our nationhood.

The stage has not come yet to think of imposition of Martial Law Administration. However, that provision, having been exercised by no less a democrat than Nehru himself, need not be a self-inflicted anathema. Considering the disease decades long and yet spreading, it would be wise to be prepared for that eventuality – in disregard of the invariable chorus of accusations, condemnation, breast-beating and rightful indignation. Time has come to stop being intimidated by the diverting clamours coming from anti-nationals, judgemental moralists, political manipulators, religious instigators and misinformed gentry, and go ahead with new approaches to prevent the falsely claimed 'Muslim' repudiation from blowing away our democratic, secular, all-inclusive way of life. As stated, preservation of national integrity needs no endorsement.

Taking firm control over the State administration through better system of governance, as discussed above, and encouragement to nationalist politics should be the sole objective to eradicate bloodbath in the Kashmir Valley. The above discussed measures, when assiduously implemented, would display India's firm intent and that would bring the majority of the people of Kashmir Valley back from the precipice of secessionism.

For Lasting Stability

Lasting stability in Kashmir Valley, and by that, in the entire State of J&K, and by implication, across the country, requires two conditions to be met. The immediate condition is to retrieve Kashmir Valley from its deep-seated anti-national indoctrination, and thus sanitise the breeding ground of secession. Popular rejection of Pakistan's incitement and the satisfaction of being Indian citizen is the best anti-dote to secessionism. The other condition arises from the fact that Pakistan would never let go of what it has decided to be its 'life-line', and desist from propagating its radical Islamist indoctrination to let the Kashmir Valley, and the rest of India, live in peace. Ultimately therefore, de-fanging of an incorrigible Pakistan and assimilation of the rest of the PoK (Western Kashmir and Gilgit-Baltistan) would have to follow a few decades or more down the line. For India, there are no other options in sight unless she reconciles to her break up against relentless – seven decades long so far – assault upon her nationhood. However, given India's current constraints, that feasibility is a long way off. Therefore, it is time to focus on the immediate measures, as discussed above, and simultaneously adopt middle term measures to rid the Kashmir Valley of its anti-national affliction.

Demographic Balancing

True assimilation of the Kashmir Valley requires undertaking of the historically practised and proved recourse, that of cultural assimilation of the local citizenry – demographic balancing, to put it starkly. To practicable extent therefore, the Valley and the rest of State should be opened for settlement of refugees, enterprising citizens and ex-servicemen, and citizens of other parts of J&K as well as that of the rest of the country. In that, for better acceptability, incentives could be offered to reward both the existing as well as settler communities and the process kept scrupulously free from religious, linguistic or ethnic chauvinism. Here too, active participation of the nation's Muslim citizens – besides the Pandits, Sikhs and other communities – would be vital; anti-nationalism injected through intrusion of radical Islamism within the Valley would have to be defeated by the sublime tenets of nationalist Islam. It would be a long haul, no doubt.

> ... State should be opened for settlement of refugees, enterprising citizens and ex-servicemen, and citizens of other parts of J&K as well as that of the rest of the country ... incentives could be offered to reward both the existing as well as settler communities and the process kept scrupulously free form religious, linguistic or ethnic chauvinism ... active articipation of the nation's Muslim citizens – besides the Pandits, Sikhs and other communities – would be vital ...

That such idea would raise the eternal objectors' alarm and petrify the orthodox, archival and condescending state functionaries, may well be appreciated, even respected, but dismissed in larger national interest – and of course, in deference to our accountability to the future generations. It is not the case that the Kashmir Valley be subject to demographic reconstruction, but the alacrity with which the option of demographic balancing is vilified may have to be calmed down if India's integrity is to be maintained. Our policy of 'segregation and pander' has failed to bear fruit in seven decades; it has in fact grown many thorns into the Indian nationhood.[19] No doubt, the Indian State's past policies have left space for a minuscule but rumbustious anti-national element to reign over the majority of peace-loving masses. This is encouragement to fascism, rooted at religious radicalism – this is not an example of democracy. The matter therefore deserves a new look.

The policy of acquiescence with socio-political expediencies, and engagement in never ending bloodbath – with measures just enough to stall secession but not enough to root it out - needs to be revised. As opined at Appendix B of this paper, arguments over the Article 370 of the Constitution need not come in the way of preservation national integrity.[20] The said Article therefore may not be a factor here, the sole factor is to preserve the nation's integrity. The question is how long would the state of tumult, ups and downs of which have already crossed the quarter century mark, permitted to bleed Kashmir? Considerations of settlement of refugees from PoK, other citizens of J&K and enterprising civilians and ex-servicemen need not therefore cause fear and alarm amongst those who are accountable to Indian history. As averred, assimilation of Kashmir Valley must necessarily be a priority campaign.

> ... not the case that the Kashmir Valley be subject to demographic reconstruction, but the alacrity with which the option of demographic balancing is vilified may have to be calmed down if India's integrity is to be maintained ... policy of 'segregation and pander' and has failed to bear fruit in seven decades ...

The First Step

While the Mujahideen-Taliban-Al Queda-Daesh inspired and radically interpreted Muslim identity has become a ground for anti-national inclinations in the Kashmir Valley, Pakistan, by its own admission, is the instigator, feeder, transporter and director of this bloody tumult – in Kashmir and to some extent, rest of India. India will find peace only when that director is disabled from wrecking its impulsive mischief. Indeed, disabling an ever-subversive Pakistan must be the conclusive step in India's mission to integrate the Kashmir Valley. In this context there are also the possibilities, even if these seem to be rather remote, that a few decades or more down the line Pakistan's obsessive incorrigibility may be cured by some development or the other, and the PoK (Western Kashmir and Gilgit-Baltistan) would find a more conducive political slot within India. But till that happens, or rather to make that happen, India needs to adopt more telling strategies even if it requires jettisoning the usual comfort of pacifist inclinations.

> ...situation has dangerous portends ... vindicating Pakistan's stance, it would generate higher and long term anguish against elimination of local boys, lead to larger spread of militancy, create life-long radicals and rebels, and give boost to infiltration, hide-out and attacks by Pakistan based terrorists ... the possibility of *Daesh* fugitives joining-in ... ominous indicators of worse days to come ... time for India to act is running out ...

During 2014–15, as the fervour of infiltration – road to certain 'martyrdom' – among Pakistan based terrorists waned, space was created for their local understudies to assume the image of Rambo *jehadis*. Even if more in form than in effect, that opportunity has attracted romantic youngsters of the Valley to don the fighters' accoutrement.[21] Resultantly, the *jehad* of radical Islam has been morphing into home grown 'freedom struggle', something that fits Pakistan's narrative to the world. Preventing security forces from eliminating these 'fighters' and 'commanders', and joining funeral marches of those killed are but the signs of community solidarity. This situation has dangerous portends. Besides vindicating Pakistan's stance, it would generate higher and long term anguish against elimination of local boys, lead to larger spread of militancy, create life-long radicals and rebels, and give boost to infiltration, hide-out and attacks by Pakistan based terrorists. Viewed under the possibility of *Daesh* fugitives joining-in, these are ominous indicators of worse days to come. Time for India to act is running out.

Having repeatedly suffered the consequences of our fissiparous afflictions in the historic past, wisdom leaves us no scope but to maintain India's firm sovereignty over that entire State at any cost. For the present, the first task is to prevent the secessionist drift that has found mooring in the Kashmir Valley. But when the first task itself remains hung incomplete over seven decades, in fact deteriorates over the past three, the situation must call for a revisit of strategies and fresh initiatives and experiments. Consistent application of contemporised approach to the problem in the Kashmir Valley, with due flexibility and sincerity, till the anti-Indian factions are squarely defeated and cleansed, must be a national goal, notwithstanding any other consideration.

*

ENDNOTES

1. Actually, there are reasons to believe that the main purpose was to perpetuate the feudal landlord-serf system of which the Muslim elite was the beneficiary. Post-partition, the system continues, more or less, in Pakistan.
2. Just as the English and the Chinese have been so even when their ruling dynasties had been of foreign origin, India has ever been a 'Hindustani' (in the larger and pristine sense of the word) nation even when ruled

by Buddhists, Muslims and Christians. In fact, the great Mogul Dynasty was native Indian in all its inheritance, and it ruled on the shoulders of both Hindu and Muslim administrators at provincial, district and down to village levels; even the military commands were of mixed composition. As for the British phobia, their Empire actually crumbled by the weight of its own domestic debilities, with the Congress movement and a palpable fear of repeat of 1857 acting as catalysts.

3. The notion of *Ummah* in itself is corrupted to suit the grip of religious bigotry over the Muslims. As the others, Muslims too are severely divided, violently at that, as indeed it is seen by the bloodletting in the entire Muslim world, Pakistan occupying the front-seat.
4. Pakistani society's ludicrous identification with Arab culture, much to the exception of its native Indian ancestry, may be an exercise to that end. Obviously, such fancies are doomed to disaster – ancestry cannot be assumed.
5. This was a period marred by felicitation of dubious candidates, rigging of elections, reward of political turn-coats, pumping of subsidies and overlook of corruption, all ending at toppling of State Government.
6. Almost all of the instigators of anti-national activism have, at one time or the other, been recipients of Government's largesse.
7. Thanks to a desire to buy appreciation, the Indian Government has kept the people of Kashmir Valley well satiated through goods and services, besides the privilege of consuming more than the average Indian. People of the Valley are thus more prosperous as compared to the rest of India and, of course, the Pakistan controlled areas. Young people, as unemployed as those in the rest of the country, but better fed and clothed, are prone to the excitements of waving rogue flags, crying for *azadi* and getting kicks from pelting stones. To them facing pellet guns is as titillating as motorbike stunts.
8. All of these wealthy and well-groomed religious 'dons' claim inheritance of the legacy of the Prophet. That allows them to impose their medieval mindsets over the Muslim masses, and to seek deferment much above their education or personal traits.
9. In Kashmir Valley, anything that has to do with non-Sunni Muslims gets targeted one way or the other: facilities for Amarnath Yatra, housing for veteran servicemen, facilitating the return of the Pandits, upkeep of Sufi shrines, appointment of people from outside the Valley, even Muslims, and the attacks anyone who might be suspected of disinclination with radical Wahabi impositions against men, women, art, music etc. – except when it suits the key manipulators of the society.

10. That the followers of Islam subscribe to many versions in theory and numerous versions in practice, that many of these are perpetually at each others' throat, and that intense intra-Muslim hatred manifests in most despicable forms of mass torture and killings, seems to escape the Kashmiri Muslim's notice. Indeed, the Kashmiri brand of sublime Islam is rejected by brainwashed bigots who claim the divinity of Islam to justify horrible acts against humanity. Sadly, Pakistan has turned into a sanctuary for such scum of humanity and an arena for their mindless bloodletting. It therefore comes as a surprise that any one in right senses would like to be a part of Pakistan when Pakistanis, who can afford to do so, are fleeing that country!
11. Observations are based from first hand discussions.
12. Inferences are culled from first hand discussions.
13. Accession of the State was ratified by the J&K Assembly in 1956 – allegedly through manipulation among Kashmiri politicians themselves!
14. PoK is 99 percent Muslim whereas India's Kashmir Valley is 95 percent so.
15. This feel comes from the fact that Indian leaders had gone out of their way to make J&K's accession as 'conditional' to the offer of plebiscite and implied autonomy, and then failed to comply.
16. The story of UN Resolution 47 of 1948/49 is interesting. It called for, as the first step, Pakistan's withdrawal of its forces from the whole of J&K, including the mercenaries of 'Azad Forces' (the post-war demobilised troops, then in Pakistan's pay roll). The second step was for India to reduce its forces till it fell to what was the minimum needed to administer the State. The third step was to hold the plebiscite under UN supervision. It is interesting to learn from records that Pakistan had sabotaged, in every manner possible, the implementation of that Resolution – the same UN Resolution that it demands to be implemented today. Pakistan knows that it would not, in fact cannot, dig out the roots it has deliberately and surreptitiously grown into the PoK, including the political, military, administrative and demographic conditions created therein over the past seven decades.
17. Ladakh is 50 percent Buddhist and 46 percent Shia Muslim – the latter are equally petrified of living under radical Sunni Pakistan. Jammu is 66 percent Hindu and 30 percent Muslim.
18. Extraordinary system of governance, on similar lines are under consideration to settle the Nagaland issue.
19. In domestic politics, concessions are liable to turn into appeasement,

followed by rise of reckless demands, as it has happened with our Reservation Policy.

20. In fact, Article 370 *inter alia* prevents Pakistan from formally and constitutionally gobbling up the PoK.
21. Elimination of the poster boy militant Burhan Wani in June 2016 was timely; it dampened the enthusiasm of many wannabes'. Also refer to *The Times of India* Report, New Delhi, 18 March, 2017.

Appendix A

CAUSES OF ANTI-NATIONAL FEELINGS IN THE KASHMIR VALLEY

Political Causes

These are as described at Part 1 of the Paper. Tutored with convincing falsifications and one-sided interpretations for Pakistan and its local minions, the Indian Government is seen as usurper of Kashmiri autonomy as promised to them, and a schemer to dilute the provisions of Article 370. Political differences of opinion have further been vitiated by a deep mistrust of the Indian Government that has been ingrained through literally door-to-door, mosque-to-mosque and madarsa-to-madarsa indoctrination – all uncontested by the State or the democratic system. Electoral frauds perpetrated by their own, and acquiesced by the Centre, has led to loss of faith on constitutional measures.

Economic Causes

(a) Poor governance and public goods and services even after the security situation had been more or less brought under control after 2001. The expected 'better days' did not materialise in an atmosphere of political manipulations.

(b) The windows of low militancy were left unexploited to bring economic progress, industrialisation, and improvement in social and essential services. The obstacles to progress – political wrestling, corruption, opportunism and internal feuds - were allowed to take centre stage against public accountability, revenue generation and work discipline. Conditions in the state almost consistently lagged behind the national growth figures.

(c) Lack of industry, abandonment of traditional handicrafts and lack of corresponding new job avenues – a universal trend, but exacerbated by local situation.

(d) Terrorism as an Industry: attraction of easy money, unaccountability against graft, loot, declining tourism. Loss of crops due to floods, cloudburst etc.

Social Causes

(a) Growth of allegiance to radical Islam against the traditional Sufi version.

(b) Indoctrination of idle youth by radical agent provocateurs has contributed to painting the usual deficiencies in education, health care, employment, infrastructure development etc. as a deliberate scheme adopted by the Union.

(c) Public brainwash; even the governance deficit and living difficulties imposed by breakdown of law and order is attributed, not to militancy, but to Indian Government. Curfews, frisking, search, alleged violation of human rights sensitivities etc. have been cleverly diverted to raise popular angst against the Indian State.

(d) Fear of religious restrictions against fundamentalist impositions. This is a case of self-infliction, as evidenced in Pakistan and parts of Middle East, that the Indian social system has failed to highlight.

(e) Historical distortions in the education curricula.

External Factors

Pakistan, helped by Islamist funding from Middle East has adopted cross-border terrorism as a profitable venture to keep the radical rascals occupied, maintain their feudalist social structure, and in the bargain keep India on the broil.

Recently Observed Factors

(a) Exploitation of social media to spread rumours and provocations.

(b) Militants finding acceptance in inciting stone-pelting mobs and addressing rallies.

(c) Attacks/threats on government officers, political representatives and policemen.

(d) Government's inability to identify and punish instigators and militant leaders.

*

Appendix B

NOTES ON ARTICLE 370

Article 370 of the Indian Constitution is a 'temporary provision' which grants special autonomous status to Jammu and Kashmir, except in matters of defence, foreign affairs, finance and communications. Application of laws enacted by the Indian Parliament in J&K requires the State Legislature's concurrence for applying all other laws.

However, over the years, much of the stated autonomy has been diluted, all in favour of Kashmiri people. Thus there is virtually no system in India that does not apply to the State of J&K. In a contrived twist the, secessionists propagate these dilutions as India's repudiation of promises made to Kashmiri people. The few but salient provisions of Article 370 that remain applicable are:

(a) Permanent residency rights are not open to rest of Indians.

(b) Declaration of emergency provisions needs the State's concurrence.

(c) Boundaries of the State are sanctified by the State Legislature.

There have been talks of revoking the Article. It is argued that this provision keeps the closed issue of the State's accession alive and encourages secessionist tendencies among Kashmiri Muslims. However, there are many literally insurmountable hurdles against doing so, including the requirement of reconvening of a new constituent assembly. Such an assembly will actually consist of leaders from the State of J&K.

However, if so intended, constitutional restrictions have never prevented any state from doing what it considers as beneficial. There will always be a way out – practically and legally. Point however is that Article 370 does not prohibit bringing about developments and peace, nor is it closed to reinterpretation with popular consent, of course. On the other hand, abrupt questions on the continuation of this Article at the current stage may start another bout of unrest, including in among the activist fraternity. It will offer an excuse to Pakistan to castigate India while overtly gobbling up the already usurped PoK.

*

INDEX

About Vivekananda International Foundation

Vivekananda International Foundation (VIF) is a non-partisan institute for dialogue on national concerns, analyses of policy options and management of challenging issues from a nationalist perspective. It is an assembly of some of India's leading expert in the fields of national security, military, diplomacy, governance, etc. who have committed under the aegis of the institute to generate ideas and stimulate actions for greater national security and prosperity.

Independently funded, VIF is not aligned to any political party or business house. Neither is it committed to any defined line of thinking but to remain cognisant to what its nationally and internationally venerated members consider to be the best for national good and best governance. It performs its charter through regular confabulations with globally regarded think tanks and venerated thinkers of the time, both national and global. Well regarded among leading think tanks, the Foundation also organises regular interactions with key policy makers of various nations with the purpose of promoting mutual understanding, strengthening friendship and reconciling differences.

Vivekananda International Foundation
3 San Martin Marg, Chanakyapuri
New Delhi-110021, India
Email: info@vifindia.org
Follow us @VIFINDIA
www.vifindia.org